CORRIDO · de
COCAINE

I wish this was only a story,
But, mister, this is the truth.

—ANTONIO AGUILAR
"The Ballad of Lamberto Quintero"

CORRIDO · de COCAINE

Inside Stories of Hard Drugs, Big Money and Short Lives

❖

Arturo Carrillo Strong

Photographs by David Burckhalter

Foreword by Charles Bowden

Harbinger House

TUCSON • NEW YORK

HARBINGER HOUSE, INC.
Tucson, Arizona

∞

This book was printed on acid-free, archival-quality paper
Typeset in 12/15 Linotron 202 Bodoni Book
Designed by Paul Mirocha

Library of Congress Cataloging-in-Publication Data

Strong, Arturo Carrillo, 1930–
Corrido de cocaine : inside stories of hard drugs, big money
and short lives / by Arturo Carrillo Strong; with a foreword
by Charles Bowden; photographs by David Burckhalter.
     p.   cm.
ISBN 0-943173-57-4 : $17.95
1. Drug traffic—Arizona—Tucson   I. Title.
HV5833.T78S76   1990
363.4 ' 5 ' 09791776-dc20   89-20032

To Josie,
who lived every good
and bad moment with me,
who never lost the faith
and gave me the strength to go on.
My partner for life,
my lover, my wife,
and my best friend.

CONTENTS

THE NARC WHO NEVER CAME IN FROM THE COLD

I HAD THIS OFFICE IN AN OLD house in the wino belt and I worked there day and night putting out a magazine. Sometimes around two or three in the morning I'd hear bums crawling around under the floorboards trying to get warm in the dirt cellar. They made soft sounds, like pigeons fluttering in a coop. A block away, the hookers would be patrolling for that last customer before the threat of dawn swept the streets clean. It was an odd magazine being published in an odd place, and a lot of odd people would drift in at all hours. That's how I met Art Strong.

He was very neat and exact, the pants pressed, the beard carefully trimmed, the shoes polished, and the smile ready. I am sitting at a folding table confronting a heap of manuscripts I have not read, a pile that seemed to grow magically each day. I hear a creaking of the floorboards, and there he is, with this fat bundle of pages in his hand. So I read them, tales of the way the barrio once was, long asides about vanished restaurants, all-night haunts, twisted street people. And about his grandfather, a lot about his grandfather. For Art is a Carrillo—Arturo Carrillo Strong—and the strands of his family's long presence in this desert course through his writing and his thoughts and his life. I remember in that first fistful of pages a section on his grandfather paying local kids to fight Art, to pound the hell out of him so that he would be tough. Tough enough to carry the name Carrillo.

Within a day or two, more pages arrived. Tales of hookers, fences, athletes, junkies, dealers, good cops, crooked cops, holidays, dogs, customs, recipes, pioneers, enemies. Nights of violence, nights of love. Bolt by bolt, he was delivering to me the tapestry of the barrio, a kind of offhanded history of how people had lived and frolicked and died.

We became friends. I think he enjoyed flogging me for all the real and imagined sins of Anglo culture. And I was perfectly suited for this task, being as ignorant as a pig about Hispanic culture, helpless in a Spanish conversation, and lacking any of the grace or flair of your basic card-carrying Latino. I was, and am, your standard pasty-faced lout. But his wife Josie made up for a multitude of Art's sins. Besides being a great cook, she was a person of warmth and grace, an antidote to the cargo of anger Art carried around inside himself. So I would sit over at their home with a plate of chili and frijoles, a homemade tortilla in my hand, and see Josie smile and hear Art's bitter words about what was going on in his hometown, and what was not being said publicly about it.

Sometimes being friends with him could be odd. One day he called me up and said he needed a favor, needed to store some things in my office. Sure. A few minutes later he showed up with shotguns, rifles, and pistols, a small armory of weapons. A guy he knew, he explained, a local dealer, owned these *armas* and right now he could not have them around his place—you know, problems and such like—and so, would I mind storing them for a while? I remember my business partner watching the armloads of guns—they certainly looked mightier than the pen—being trundled into my office, and he turned to me and said, "I don't even want to know." But, of course, one thing I liked about Art was he did want to know.

He'd been born here, his family went back more than a century— a local public school is named Carrillo—and through blood, friendships, or work, he was tied into a seemingly endless network of Mexican Americans and Sonorans. He'd worked in the family mortuary, been a cop for years, spent a long time as a narc, run a restaurant. He had the perfect background for being the official historian of the barrio, the man who knew the real event that inspired the *corridos* that blasted from the jukeboxes. But more importantly, he had the eye. Somehow, Art had become obsessed with getting it all down. He'd bought one of the first personal computers when they came out and had begun writing, writing without an audience or a clue about the habits of newspapers and magazines and publishers. He'd just started writing.

And, like I said, he had that eye. For a while, I'd worked for a newspaper, and the main thing I learned was that most people are born blind and prefer to remain in that condition. He once brought me this piece about a bunch of hookers who pounded the pavement on a stretch of the South Side and each afternoon they'd gather at a fence's house and watch "Hawaii Five-O" together. Each time the heroes would make a bust, they'd shout, "Book'm Danno!" And when the program ended, they'd plunge out into the life of the city to fuck and suck businessmen on their way home from the office. For Art, and for me, these afternoons of television watching did not have any larger meaning. And, thank God, they were not a symbol. They simply were. And so I printed it.

He also had contacts, as any reader of this book will soon discover. In a nation where everyone moves once a month and marriages last only slightly longer than one-night stands, Art spoke for a community of Mexican Americans that seemed rooted into the ground like ancient mesquite trees. He wouldn't just know the hooker, he would know the hooker's father. And when it came to the drug trade, his fingers could trace veritable family trees of junkies and dealers coursing for generations through the community. On the flip side, he'd also know the rancher, the priest, the activist, the cop. And he sensed that this world he knew so well was being ignored, buried alive by a white world of newspapers, magazines, and nice scholarly books that usually failed to notice that it even existed. He lived in a city that boasted of its bicultural heritage while busy denying or bulldozing half of that culture. He intended somehow to right that wrong, to get it all down. I remember one day he came to me with these fat photo albums that had been kept up by a minor fence on the South Side for over thirty years. The guy, for reasons he probably did not understand himself, had taken photos of every hooker who had ever worked a particular stretch of the South Side. The images were eerie—women with beautiful faces and ancient eyes, junkies nodding off after that blissful fix, young, almost girlish faces smiling into the camera with their blouses off. Many of the people in the album were already dead. I didn't know what to do with the albums and neither did Art. But we both sensed they mattered. Someone else, at least, was trying to keep score, trying to get it all down.

And then, of course, there was the matter of the drugs.

◆ ◆ ◆

To a lot of people, Art back then might have seemed crazed by drugs. But not to me, since I was similarly crazed. Tucson had always had drugs, the border being so near, but in the late seventies and early eighties the life changed and got harder and bloodier. Sonorans moved into the local action and crushed the guys in the barrio. And then, because of federal pressure on the cocaine business in Florida, the pathways shifted, and suddenly Tucson was in a major corridor for all the drugs coming north. People started dying. Quite a few people.

None of this seemed to come to the notice of the local newspapers. There would be small items on the back pages about a body found, a shooting reported. And then an enormous silence. Once Art and I had lunch with a homicide detective. We were sitting there slurping bowls of soup in a barrio hangout when Art casually asked how many drug-related killings the cop had tallied so far for the year. The man paused and reflected for a moment, and allowed there'd been maybe three or four. I think at that moment Art and I both suddenly understood the rules: Unless you left a message stapled to a body stating in clear English that this was a drug killing, it would not be counted as such. Bad for business, bad for the town's image, bad for the department.

I had the same problem at the magazine where I was constantly told that people did not want to hear about this kind of stuff, that we couldn't print endless sad stories. And besides, they'd say, the last issue was too brown, too much about Mexicans. Of course.

Sometimes in the late afternoon, Art and I would wind up in a bar. He'd be in one of those cold furies that seem to seize him at times like a summer storm. His voice would be controlled, his face impassive, his hand clutching a Seagram's Seven. He would not get drunk, he was too angry for that. The booze would seem to vanish into some black hole in his soul. And he would start saying he was going to give up, to stop writing. That no one cared, that nobody gave a damn. And sometimes for weeks he would stop writing.

But these moments would pass. Suddenly, after one of these storms, he'd show up with a hundred pages, pages about a milkman who clawed his way out of poverty, or a contract killer, or the way Christmas used to be in the barrio, or about the curious breed of dogs people kept when he was a kid. One time he was over at my house in the evening and we were having a beer and swapping lies. I guess he got bored with my brilliant wit, so while I went to the kitchen to find another beer, he turned on my computer and started writing. Then he went home and left the story behind like a kind of finger exercise. I still have it:

Domingo's Ghostly Love Affair

The way Domingo told it, he was working on a big construction job as a diesel mechanic near Flagstaff, Arizona, when he met her. It was around 1976 or 1978, the bar was too much like the hundreds of bars where he'd wasted his hard-earned money trying to kill a few hours. He felt stupidly drunk when he staggered out to his car. The next thing he heard was the horn blaring and then he felt a gentle tug that pulled him away from the steering wheel. She was beautiful, she was wearing a diaphanous white dress with what seemed like a lot of veils. She smiled and pointed to the policeman on duty outside of the bar. "Let me drive you home so you don't get arrested," she told him.

Domingo's trailer was only a few blocks away; she parked the car and they went inside. It was the best sex he'd ever had; after they were through she went to the small kitchen, opened the ice box and made Domingo a fantastic breakfast. The second time was even better, and as they lay in bed she told him she was married. Her husband, she said, worked at the Texaco station just outside of town, but as long as she was home before six in the morning, there wouldn't be any trouble. A few minutes before six it was still dark as she directed him through the narrow streets. There was an eerie fog lying over the cold ground, and when she pointed to where she lived, he couldn't really see the house. They kissed, she promised to see him again soon, and then she was gone.

He looked for landmarks: the large oak tree across from the meadow, the gabled roof and the living ocotillo fence— all he needed if he ever had to find her house again. Right now he felt too damn good. The next few weeks were filled with hard work and overtime to finish out the contract. On the last day, before they were scheduled to pack up and go home, Domingo went back to the bar. He waited for her, asked the bar maids and the regulars if they had seen her. No one knew what the hell he was talking about. After the regular company had left, Domingo stayed on and drove to the Texaco station where she said her husband worked.

And of course the gas station was boarded up, had not been in business for years, and so forth. That place where the house had been hidden in the fog turned out to be a cemetery.

That was when I began to understand that Art was essentially a junkie. The streets of the barrio were his drug of choice, writing his favorite technique for injecting the life into his veins. He is not a writer searching for material. He is a human archive frantically trying to get it all down before it disappears. He is going to be the man who proves things actually happened, that people actually lived, that communities the city fathers and planners barely believe exist actually have histories, legends, and arcs of triumph and defeat of biblical proportions. And he's going to do it the way any cop would—by patiently building his case.

This book is a product of those days of frustration when no one would print what Art saw and heard. In fact no one even wanted to know what he was learning. It is an odd book. This is not a government study, outlining The Problem and then ticking off the master plan that will solve it to the tune of a couple of billion dollars. Nor is it a scholarly history fat with footnotes, jargon, and categories. It's a lot like life, messy, attractive, driven, and full of voices, scents, and passions. And it's probably unique. Here, for once, you'll hear the accounts of the people in the life—not talking to their parole officers, but just talking. They're talking about how to cut a deal in Miami. How to kill. What it is like to be tortured. What all that money can buy. Why people go into the life, and why almost no one ever gets out, alive.

A lot of it concerns Mexicans and Mexican Americans. I suppose if Colombia happened to be north of Canada, somebody in North Dakota would be writing a similar book full of the voices of dealers from the Great White North. But maybe not. People like Art Strong are not that thick. I edited that strange magazine where I first met him for about three years, and I never did have another Art Strong come in the door. Most people aren't very curious about life, and if they are curious, they're lazy, and if they're not lazy, they're careful. Careful people don't learn what Art learned. And even if you meet someone who is curious, energetic, and not careful, they still usually lack that final ingredient: love.

All stories are moral stories, and all moral stories must be rooted in love. These chronicles contain the history of a community under siege and they're the work of a man who loves both the community and the siege. They are the story, in a way, of the narc who never came in from the cold. The information was not easy to come by. People in the life are not too gabby about their activities. And distrust is often expressed through homicide. What you will read in this book is the result of endless conversations, contacts, and whispers. The people talking required months or years of cultivating before they decided to speak. And in the end, they're not likely to talk at all unless you are from the barrio and are of the blood and know someone who can vouch for you. A lot of things written about the drug world are based on the files of various police agencies and concern the work of people in those agencies. Not this book.

Once when Art and I were in a border town tracking the history of a contract killer who had butchered a couple of dozen people, we were steered to a keymaker who operated from the back of his truck. The truck was a little unusual for Mexico—it had a nice color television and a big comfortable lounge chair—but then so was the keymaker, a big, beefy guy with gold chains dripping from his neck and a fat Rolex watch with a gold band and diamonds spelling out his name. We never asked what he charged for his product. After a couple of visits, he was keen to help us and took us to visit a cop who knew many details about our assassin. Our keymaking guide went up to the cop's door on a dusty side street and talked to the man's wife, who said he could not speak, he was hung over. We came back later, again and again. But the cop—who, not surprisingly, was a participant in the life—never would talk to our keymaker friend or to us. He was afraid, too frightened to even come to the door. Someone in the town had spoken foolishly about the assassin we were interested in and had been promptly killed a month or two before. In the end, we squandered two days and never got past the cop's front door on that side street. This book is about the doors that did open.

To do this kind of work, you must have the appetite. I remember one afternoon when Art came into my office with his recorder and insisted I listen to a tape. Suddenly voices and street sounds filled the room, the dealer sitting on his front steps, the guy walking down the street who'd just got out of the joint and needed five for a six-pack, the quick comments and clipped sentences of deals and bad times. His eyes gleamed with pleasure as the tape rolled. It was all so alive, it was all right there. It was happening right now, and someone had to get it down. A record must be made. Attention must be paid.

And so Arturo Carrillo Strong did that necessary work.

CHARLES BOWDEN

PREFACE

WORKING YOUR FIRST DRUG CASE is like going on a first date. You're scared, excited, full of anticipation, an unforgettable experience. The adrenaline rush is incredible and keeps you high for hours. The possibilities for error are so great that it's almost impossible not to make a mistake. The world of the undercover cop is a make-believe world, so some mistakes are allowed.

What makes it fascinating is the element of danger, the matching of wits in a chess game where the pawns are real people. You're going one-on-one with a sinister character who's dealing drugs; it might be in an alley or in a house full of junkies, but it always goes down in a room that reeks of paranoia. Making the deal and playing the role engulfs you—it's like playing cops and robbers when you were a kid, except that now the bad guys have real guns.

Then you come back to the real world. You walked into a nest of snakes and somehow got out without being bitten. Maybe that's why some cops do it and love it, the excitement, the thrill of it, the forces of good battling evil. Afterwards it's almost an out-of-body experience. You see yourself walking back to your partner, driving back to the office and handing the chief the paper of heroin you just bought.

You watch yourself making out the report, remembering every detail, reliving the moment on paper so when you go to court, the defense attorney won't make you look like too much of a jerk.

Then you're back inside yourself, and, the best part, the camaraderie takes over. The job is done and you go to a cops' bar to unwind. Then, and only then, do you go home and tell your new bride all about it. The next day it all starts again, playing the part. You're young and loving every minute of it.

At some point, I imagine, every cop who has worked the street day after day becomes weary of the ugliness and misery he must contend with. I know the feeling. Your mind becomes saturated with the things you are seeing, things you never knew existed outside your straight world. There is a feeling for the rest of your life that all you want to see and hear and think about are the good things.

Before you know it, it's over, and you turn in your badge. It feels like losing a friend. You miss the comfortable feel of a gun on your hip. The party's over, but you don't want to go home. It's time to move on to bigger and better things, forget the bad, remember the good, and then convince yourself it was only a job. You find out it isn't that easy. It's hard to stay away. You start saving clippings, storing information that you're probably never going to use.

One day, in a barbershop that never left the past, you meet up with the guy you made that first buy from, your first case, and it's like going to your high-school reunion. For some reason he tells you what's coming down on the street, who's moving junk on what corner. He tells you about things you have no business knowing, and that old itch comes back. Like every ex-cop you think you ought to write a book, that your story is unique and has to be told, when all along it's every cop's story.

I'm always asked why these people who are former or active drug addicts and drug dealers talk to me. What is it they want out of this? At least two, and maybe three, of the characters in the book are still in the business of selling drugs. Some of them might be risking their lives talking the way they do. A couple are possibly one good connection away from returning to the old life. Why would they tell me what their lives in drugs were like? It's a very difficult question to answer without sounding like a blowhard.

Maybe it's because I've always been part of the landscape. The barrios were my backyard, and my life and the lives of some of the characters have intertwined since we were kids. There's an element of trust involved. The street has a way of checking you out that is probably as efficient, if not more so, than any internal-affairs investigation. You have to know the language of the street and be able to reach that level comfortably, be their equal, so to speak. You have to know what to ask and when to stop asking. You never threaten, you never beg. It's not the question, it's how you ask it. Then there's the ego; there certainly has to be a great deal of ego involved, both on my part and on the part of those who wanted their side of the story told.

The people who talked to me in this book wanted to be heard. They were trying to say that they feel pain, sorrow, happiness—and sometimes regrets for what they are or were. I don't intend to condemn anyone, nor do I condone what they do. I felt people should know how the other half lives, not only the junkies and the dealers but also the cops who fight the spread of drugs.

What emerges can't be told by statistics. The solution to the problem of drugs is evasive and far too complex for a street cop, but maybe what it's going to take is a simple solution. The arguments for and against legalization of certain drugs are many and freely given. I asked a drug dealer what would happen if we legalized drugs. "I'd be fucked," he said. Is that the answer? I don't know. I think so, but we'll never know unless we try, and we probably never will.

CORRIDO · de
COCAINE

The people, times, and places depicted in this book are real;
only the names of some of the characters have been changed to
protect the guilty. They must remain anonymous on these pages,
or else they might disappear in reality—forever.

1 EL PADRINO DE COCAINE[†]

*The police will lock you up and take
away your money, but they have to
feed you and take care of you, while
the people involved with drugs will
take away your money, torture
you in the cruelest manner imaginable,
and then take away your life.*

—Emiliano

THE SONORAN SUN SEEMS FIXED
at its midday high point, stalled in the sky over the creature hanging
by his wrists from the tall horse-training post in the sandy courtyard.
He is barefooted, stripped to the waist, and tied to the training ring
with leather thongs, his arms raised above his head so that he
cannot sit.

After the second day he stopped worrying about the blisters and
the sloughing skin of his back and stomach. When the third day had
passed, Emiliano looked forward to dying, prayed for death.

He had no idea what the hell was going on, why they have treated
him this way after all of the years they have been in business
together. Time has stopped meaning anything to him. Is it two days,
three, a week since he arrived and was taken at gunpoint? When was
the last time they gave him water? At least the excruciating pain in
his wrists and shoulders has stopped. Now there is only a dull ache.

Crazy dreams enter his mind and he tries to smile, knowing he
can't because his lips won't cooperate. Over and over this thought
keeps coming back—when they finally cut him down he will be over

[†]The Godfather of Cocaine

six feet tall and his arms will dangle to the ground. It would be fine
to be six feet tall instead of five-foot-five.

If only Geraldo or Ernesto would come out and tell him why he
deserves this kind of punishment. The only one who has talked to
him is a baby-faced, cat-eyed little bastard with skinny arms, deli-
cate hands, and a cold stare. Emiliano knows him, he is Geraldo's
bodyguard and *gatillero*, or hit man.

For eight years Emiliano has been buying his cocaine from them.
In all that time he has never missed a payment or failed to sell the
entire shipment. Bastards. He is a man of respect, he is Emiliano
Carranza, the Godfather of Cocaine in the great city of Tucson in the
United States of America. Had not the police themselves given him
the title by which every man of importance in the drug trade knows
him? They have no right to treat him like a peasant caught with his
hands in the *frijole* pot of his neighbor's woman. The least they could
do is come out and kill him like a man. They hang him here like a
goat ready to be butchered for the pit.

The sun is overhead always, and the buzzards with their wrinkled
red necks and white-tipped wings soar closer and closer while he
grows weaker and weaker. What he wouldn't give to have the .22
rifle he owned when he was a boy. He curses the Mexican sky that
can't even produce one cloud to cover the goddamn Mexican sun.

Emiliano is sure now that it has been just three days since he
arrived at Ernesto's ranch to meet with his partner Geraldo and find
out what happened to the cocaine they were supposed to have delivered two weeks earlier, and what happened to the money. Why does
Geraldo's baby-faced killer keep insisting that no one has shown up
to pay for the coke? He tells Emiliano over and over that they want
their money. No, not just the money, they want him to suffer as an
example to others who might think of cheating Geraldo and Ernesto.

He sees Geraldo and his *gatillero* come out of the house. Geraldo
sits in his large wicker chair under the wide veranda. With tall
glasses of ice water and shot glasses of tequila filling their hands,
they look at him and shake their heads at his shame.

In the early morning of the seventh day, Geraldo and his *gatillero* come from the kitchen and stand before Emiliano, still picking their teeth for bits of the eggs and cured ham grown right here on the ranch. Emiliano pictures a plate of eggs and ham generously covered with fresh green salsa and a side dish of refried beans. The thought of what they have just eaten tortures him, the breakfast aromas crowd the air around him. With the last bit of strength left in him, Emiliano straightens his weary legs and stands to face them.

"Emiliano, my friend, why have you betrayed me?" Geraldo whispers softly.

Carranza tries to speak, but all that comes out is an awful croaking sound that startles them, a voice he himself does not recognize as human. They stare at him and he at them for what seems like a very long time. Finally Geraldo shakes his head sadly and tells the *gatillero*, "Kill him. Put him out of his misery."

The gun appears in the killer's hand as if by magic. It seems too large for his small hand, but he handles the gun as if it were part of him. But after the hours spent in torture and interrogation, prisoner and captor have become closer than most men do in years of knowing each other. As is often the case, a bond seems to have grown between Emiliano Carranza and his tormentor.

"Why don't you kill me yourself, or aren't you man enough to kill an innocent man face to face?" Emiliano hears himself speaking to Geraldo in a voice that is more a growl.

"Kill him!" shouts Geraldo.

"No, I think he is telling the truth. He too has been betrayed. Here is my gun, you kill him." In one motion the gun in the killer's hand reverses itself, the grip pointed at Geraldo.

From the shadows of the veranda a voice booms out toward the three men. "That's enough! Cut him down and bring him inside."

In the corrals and the surrounding trees men lay aside automatic weapons and rush toward him. He feels more than sees the glint of steel and the razor-sharp blade cutting through the leather thongs that have become a part of him. They drag him into the house, and his legs feel as though they belong to someone else. The bed where the *vaqueros* place him has been made up with silk sheets, the room is dark, and he feels the coolness of the thick adobe walls. Later the women remove his tattered pants and treat his skin with herbs from the desert. And finally a few drops of cool water trickle down his throat.

As long as he lives he will never forget the voice of Ernesto coming from the shadows of the veranda. He had not arrived a moment too soon, and somehow Emiliano had known all along that it was not his old friend Ernesto who was doing this to him.

On the second day after his release Emiliano awakes to the sound of running water. It is early afternoon, and from the bathroom he hears women laughing, then soft giggling sounds. The doorway is filled by a woman in a long skirt and a colorful peasant blouse. She is large and round with sparkling black eyes full of laughter, and her long black hair is tied back into a bun. The two women with her are young and beautiful and all three have the slightly slanted eyes and dark skin of the *campezina*, the ranch woman of Mexico. At first they smile at his nakedness, then, with eyes averted, leave the room while he slips into the warm scented water of his bath.

From the courtyard Emiliano hears the sound of mariachi music and the laughter of friends meeting once more to party—Mexican style. Staring back at him from the mirror in the bathroom is a miserable shadow of his once handsome face, now gaunt and more deeply tanned than ever. His beard, which he usually keeps so well trimmed, is now ragged and flecked with gray. When he leaves the bathroom he feels better, his beard and moustache trimmed, his body rid of the awful smell of himself. On the bed he finds his white suit laid out and pressed, the vest hanging from one of the bedposts. In the closet he finds his white armadillo boots.

When he walks out into the courtyard, he is greeted by cheers and wolf whistles from the many guests who have already arrived at the invitation of Ernesto and Geraldo. The two drug lords walk toward Emiliano and embrace him gently to show one and all that everything is forgiven. In attendance are the most important drug mafiosos of Mexico. The hacienda has many bedrooms, and most will stay for the fiesta in honor of Emiliano Carranza as long as the party runs. In the large sunken *sala,* or living room, the furniture is massive. The walls are lined with big-game heads taken in the wilds of the Sierra Madre on the legendary hunting trips staged by Ernesto. A large round coffee table in the center of the room is loaded with trays containing marijuana cigarettes, cocaine, and various types of uppers and downers.

The women lounging on the deep sofas and standing around talking to the men in the next *sala* are all young and beautiful, and they have only one purpose at this fiesta, to please the guests with their beauty and favors. By the end of the second day Emiliano has all but forgotten his ordeal—except that he will never be able to face a horse again without remembering the training post in the courtyard. The fiesta will last for seven days and nights, or until the last guest is ready to call it quits.

On the last night of the fiesta Emiliano meets face to face with the baby-faced killer. He does not have a name, only a title in Emiliano's mind: *gatillero,* triggerman. They face each other and stare for several seconds, Emiliano smiles, and the *gatillero* offers his hand. Emiliano pushes it away and embraces him instead. After all, the man was just doing his job. Business is business.

♦   ♦   ♦

There was no telling how the interview would go. On the phone he wanted to talk about his love of art and the work he's been doing to create a showplace for his art in one of the rooms of his house. I want to talk about drugs and what it's like being Tucson's "Godfather of Cocaine." Visions of wild parties, serving plates filled with cocaine, heroin, and marijuana come to mind. The house on the south side of town where he lives sticks out like a sore thumb, not because it is extraordinary or fabulous compared to houses in other parts of Tucson, but because the neighborhood is very old and most of the homes that surround it are so poor. The police report called the house a fortress, but except for some wrought-iron doors and wooden frames around the Spanish-style arched windows I couldn't see any of the things that would make it a fortress, like concertina wire on top of electrified fences.

I often hear stories about Emiliano Carranza and his house, about secret panels, hidden rooms, about the wildcat he keeps to guard the house and the cellar where there are from one to forty bodies buried, according to who is telling the story. Are the police still keeping him under surveillance? Will my license-plate number be stored in someone's computer for all eternity? The house seems innocent enough in the morning sun, the gates are open, and I don't see any armed guards patrolling the perimeter with Uzis at the ready. Try as I might, I can't locate any undercover cops posing as telephone, gas, or electric repairmen lurking nearby. The driveway is empty, so I pull in and park under a palm tree. I notice the front screen door is ajar, and to my left is a guest house that appears to have been vacant for some time. Force of habit from thirteen years as a cop makes me look around the grounds for a handy exit. Several citrus trees in full bloom dot the large front yard, and I can't help but notice that there isn't one blade of grass, no weeds, on the table-top smoothness of the dirt yard. It comes to mind that nobody can walk around the house without leaving footprints.

From the yard, reluctant to venture too far away from my truck, I call out. Nobody answers my hellos or nervous whistle. Finally I approach the house, climb the steps, and notice that the front door leading into the living room is also open, as if someone has left in a big hurry and isn't worried about anyone bothering the house.

Turning to leave, I feel neither disappointment nor anger at being stood up. A young voice from within brings me back. A teenager appears at the open door, fifteen or sixteen I judge, fairly tall but overweight with a pleasant round face and a warm smile. His dark brown hair is slicked down and wavy, still wet from a recent shower.

"Are you Arturo?" he asks. Before I can answer he goes on, "My father will be right back, he said for you to come in and sit down." His name is Carlos, he tells me politely, and he offers me something to drink and some cookies even before we go inside.

I notice the steps leading up to the wraparound front porch, covered with expensive Mexican tile. The porch that protects the front of the house from the sun and rain is partly enclosed with screen. The heavy wrought-iron door is painted white, and the screen around the lock is ripped. The possibilities of how it was torn leap around in my head. The porch walls are painted with garish murals of South Sea scenes, palm trees, and water fowl. The house appears to be under constant repair, as if someone is always patching, fixing, or changing the configuration of the building. The living room is small, a large Panasonic TV with a curved screen occupies one corner. Soft chairs are scattered about the room, not fancy, not ragged, not what I expected a rich drug dealer would own.

It feels strange sitting in a drug dealer's (or, as he claims, a former drug dealer's) house waiting for him to come home. I have always been on the outside looking in. I sink deeper into the chair and can't help but wonder what the thick adobe walls would tell me about this house if they could speak.

Carlos comes back from the kitchen with a tray containing a steaming cup of coffee and some cookies. He missed school today because his father had to go to the bus station to pick up someone coming in from Mexico and he can't leave the house alone.

I hear a car pull into the driveway. The Godfather is home. I had hoped to get better acquainted with Carlos, maybe find out something about his father. In a few minutes he bounces into the room wearing white running shorts, a white sleeveless T-shirt, and high-top running shoes. The face, beard, and long hair have not changed much from the picture on the front page of the *Arizona Daily Star* in 1984 that showed him being led away by a police sergeant after his arrest in a million-dollar cocaine bust. The hair seems grayer, the body slimmer, the eyes still alert, still defiant.

The smile comes easily and the handshake is firm. There are good vibes immediately. Then another disappointment—the guest from Mexico turns out to be a teenage boy not much older than Carlos. He appears to be nervous and more than a little scared. Emiliano motions for me to follow him and the boy jumps up after us. One gesture from Emiliano stops him practically in midair, and he sits down quickly.

The door leads to a narrow stairway and down into the most unbelievable room in all of Tucson, if not in the entire Southwest. The walls are painted in bright colors: one wall is royal blue, one cardinal red, another gold. The ceiling, a combination of gold and white. Over the door leading to the side street there is a large crest with the words, "The Realm of Carranza." Gold-painted ceramic lions guard every corner. To Emiliano lions represent male authority and are fierce defenders of their pride. Gold filigree borders the doors, the windows, the ceiling. In the center of the room a glass chandelier hangs from the ceiling beneath a hand-painted mural of angels encircled by more gold filigree, giving the room the feel of a cathedral. On the north wall a group of closetlike openings that very much resemble church confessionals without the customary drapes occupies the entire wall. In the space to the right a marble statue of an angel, with only a gold sash covering its naked body, stands in a niche carved into the wall.

The angel, he tells me, was stolen from a cemetery in Mexico. A friend spotted the statue on a nameless grave and knew immediately that the angel was made for Emiliano. He broke it off at the base and smuggled the reluctant angel across the border and gave it to Emiliano. The bar located on the west end of the room is simple in design, only the red, blue, and gold decorations distinguish it. A photo album at one end of the marble top catches my eye. There aren't any bottles of liquor visible, but three empty beer cans testify that the bar is functional. Emiliano goes behind the bar and leans on the wide smooth surface; he has a pleased smile as he looks over his realm. I notice that there are only two chairs in the room—no, not really chairs but thrones, covered in red velvet, the arms and legs painted gold. The chairs face the large arched window that is recessed from the outside wall and contains a marble fountain without water. The chair to the right is high backed, the king's throne; the one to the left obviously belongs to the queen. Both are protected by a gold rope to discourage anyone from sitting in them. So I stand.

A phone rings in another part of the house and he excuses himself, telling me to make myself at home. At the northeast corner I notice a set of stairs that lead down into the basement. I try to ignore them, try not to think about the stories of men who have entered this house never to be seen again. The cellar calls me. The door is ajar, there is a dim light coming from below, but I will have to go down several steps to see anything. My imagination plays tricks on me. I think I smell fresh earth. Footsteps from above dissuade me from going down any farther and I retreat to stand by the bar.

When Carranza returns, he gives me the tour-guide spiel as he leads me around the room, explaining in detail the meaning of each filigree design. The room becomes transformed in his eyes into a grand ballroom with high ceilings and marble floor. He describes the beautiful ladies in long dresses and the gentlemen wearing high-necked uniforms that he sees dancing to a Viennese waltz in his room. Yet, despite the ardor of his speech, he doesn't come across as a madman. This room filled with what he calls "his art" has consumed him, his time, money, and labor, for several years. Four of his wives have become so jealous of this room that they have walked out on him. One has tried several times to have him killed and was responsible for his last arrest.

Is he really crazy? The thought runs through my mind, but I am determined to hear him out. Why is he willing to give up the women he loves, the mother of his children, his lovers, and all who stand in the way of his passion? He knows that very few will enjoy this kind of "art." To most it is ugly. He admits in a whisper that his four wives have all told him this. Even his stepmother, who seems to love him deeply, has told him this and calls him *mi hijo tonto*, my dumb son, though she says it lovingly. He accepts being called her dumb son and admits it's dumb to feel this way about his collection. But I sense he doesn't want me to agree.

The initial impression of his masterpieces is that they are beautiful and valuable, but they do not withstand close scrutiny. The cheapness comes through. He senses my feelings and changes the subject. To my astonishment he can neither read nor write, has never attended formal school, yet he made and lost more money than most of us will see in a lifetime. Some he made honestly by the sweat of his brow, the natural skills in his hands, his nimble mind. Most he made selling cocaine and marijuana, by receiving stolen property, and by organizing criminals to do his bidding. He confesses he doesn't believe in anything religious, in God or the church or the hereafter. He has no fear of going to hell, nor does he expect a reward in heaven. He has faith only in himself and the love of his stepmother.

Emiliano does believe there is power, both good and evil, and he firmly believes that certain people have these powers and will not hesitate to use them against him if he isn't alert and stronger than they are. He believes that his stepmother, Paulita Carranza, a full-blooded Yaqui Indian, has these powers and can protect him. At first he is reluctant to talk about her, but somehow I persuade him that it's important.

♣ When my stepmother was only a child living in a tiny Sonoran village near Hermosillo, she says she discovered that she had certain powers of healing, and soon the entire village found out about her and started coming to her when they were sick or injured. The village was also the home of Gallego, the most powerful *brujo blanco*, or white witch, in all of Sonora. She became his only student and protégé, because there could only be one heir to the power he holds. The lessons were long and time consuming and not without physical pain to both the teacher and student. There is, according to her, a transfer of power from teacher to pupil. Sometimes she desperately wanted to stop learning the art. But Gallego was still stronger than her and she kept going to him.

But there came a time when she could stand no more and she had to leave Mexico. She already had many powers and her training was almost complete, but the pressure became too great and she was too tired to go on. She was young and strong, attractive in many ways, and she had been offered a job in Tucson with the family of a well-known Mexican businessman. She met my father, Faustino Carranza, and fell in love with him. They were married a short time later and she had one child from him, my half-brother, who is very close to me. When my father died, she was still my mother, and I care for her a great deal. He was very hard on his women and she shows it like all of his wives did. ✦

Emiliano apparently was the least favorite of Faustino's children. He barely remembers his natural mother, who died when he was very young. When Emiliano was only eleven years old, the family was living on the Ed Hudgings ranch in Brownsville, Texas. His father sent him up into the hills with a wagon, a few supplies, and a .22-caliber rifle to kill game to feed himself. His job was to cut and burn the thorns off the nopal cactus so the cattle could then eat it. After a month Emiliano came home only to find out that the family had moved. There was no forwarding address or any indication how to reach them. From a married sister who lived in town he found they had moved to Colorado.

Three years ago the full impact of his stepmother's powers became apparent to Emiliano and fortified his faith in her.

Emiliano is certain that one of his ex-wives is able to call on the black arts as well, and that she used this power to convince his son Carlos to try to poison his father. She then used this power on her brother, Joe Moreno, who was once Emiliano's most trusted aide.

After the failed attempt to kill him through his son, Emiliano received a call from his stepmother. He is not to leave the house for any reason until she gives him the word. He doesn't argue, it was she who warned him about the poison in the soup Carlos brought him. Across the street lives a large mangy dog that bites everyone who comes near him. For some reason the dog crosses the street and begins sleeping in the entryway by the side door of Emiliano's house. This dog has always hated him but now won't allow anyone near his house.

For three days this goes on, and on the fourth day the dog goes home. That day a neighbor comes over and tells Emiliano about the man who has been lurking by the back fence between their properties and about the dog driving him away. This is not a neighborhood-watch area and the man doesn't want to get involved. On the South Side you learn to mind your own business. Another call comes from his stepmother—it's safe to go out now. The next call is from Joe Moreno, his ex-brother-in-law, Carlos's uncle, Emiliano's trusted aide. He wants to have coffee at a small restaurant on the South Side.

"Were you going to kill me?" Emiliano wants to know as they face each other across the large table outside Mom's cafe.

"Yes, I don't know why," says Joe Moreno. "Something told me to wait for you and kill you. I didn't want to, but I had to. I had my knife and I was going to kill you. If you had come out I would have killed you. I'm sorry, I don't know what came over me. When I woke up this morning the desire to kill you was gone. Can you ever forgive me?" Tears of shame stream down his face, they embrace. For the time being Joe is not a danger to him, but that can change.

There have been seven attempts on Emiliano's life in the past three years, the latest occurring in the spring of 1989. It was Joe again, and this time he was packing a gun. Luckily, Emiliano stayed one step ahead of him. You would think Emiliano would be more careful or at least arm himself, which he claims he doesn't do because of his probation, or hire protection. "The only protection I need is my stepmother, she will take care of me," he says. He talks of his profession as though he were just another overworked executive.

✦ Over the years, when you are in this terrible business that involves so much money and greed, you have enemies whether you deserve them or not. The newspapers and writers like you write only about the fancy cars, the women, big homes, and the glamor of riding first-class in the fast lane. There is no way to describe the enormous pressure and fear that must be endured constantly by the successful mafiosos, as we are often characterized. That pressure and fear is shared with the family along with the profits, and so the wife and children are tarred by the same brush. The successful drug dealer is less concerned with the police than he is with others in the same business. The police will lock you up and take away your money, but they have to feed you and take care of you, while the people involved with drugs will take away your money, torture you in the cruelest manner imaginable, and then take away your life.

The competition is unbelievable, there isn't any diploma to sell drugs. All you need is the product and a few customers. You would be amazed at how many people try their hand at being drug dealers at least once. Basically good people who are just trying to make that extra buck to pull themselves up.

In the world I was involved in, the big time, so to speak, it is very much like the things that happened in the movie *Scarface*. Once I was in Miami, with Rene's right-hand man. Rene is one of the most powerful men in that city. We were at one of the best night clubs, a club that had three levels. The higher the level, the more it cost. Ten dollars for a glass of wine, can you believe it? We were with two ladies and just enjoying our meal when machine-gun fire broke out. The shooting was at the level below us. Two guys just walked in and wiped out two couples at the table below us. Everybody ducked, and two minutes later everything was calm again, the gunmen were gone, and the place was almost empty.

What I'm trying to say is that there is always someone trying to step up to the spot above and if you're in that spot, or they think you are, you become a target.

When I was in the business, I was able to control this with the respect I commanded. But now I'm vulnerable, and the people in this business have long memories. Maybe I offended some people or refused to sell them what they wanted or didn't trust them for the money. Who knows? ✤

The thought of his being crazy was something I never considered seriously. A little strange maybe, but not crazy. He is testing me, trying to see how far he can go before I pack up and leave. I can feel this, and he doesn't know how close he is to succeeding. Another phone call leaves me alone. The mosaic tile floors are killing my feet and I'm tempted to sit on his throne despite the gold rope, but I settle for the ledge of the window. Over the honeycomb fireplace beside me is a large oil painting of Emiliano wearing a dark suit with a vest and a matching wide-brimmed hat with the brims down front and back. He doesn't smile, it's his Godfather portrait. In the background is a white Rolls-Royce.

When he returns, he shows me the photo album that I spotted earlier on the bar. He flips the pages quickly, pictures of his wedding to Sally, the latest wife to leave him because of the art room. Sally with two young daughters. Sally who is arrested with him on his latest bust. Later she will be released and not charged, but the bust isn't the reason she leaves. It's the damn room.

Enough for one day. We have talked for two hours, but little about cocaine and the drug world in which he was once a king. I haven't seen the cellar or the wildcat, but there are rooms I have not entered.

Since that first day we have had many meetings. One that stands out in my mind included Paulita Carranza. She confirmed many of the things Emiliano mentioned about Gallego, the old *brujo blanco* she studied under. Gallego moved to Tucson a few years after Paulita came here. She assured me that it was Gallego who assumed the form of the dog to protect Emiliano. Shortly after this happened Gallego was found dead in the rubble of his burned-out shack in old Pasqua Village.

There were times when she opened up to me and was warm and friendly. There were other times when she was concerned only about how much money her son would realize from this "interview business." On one occasion she told me about her friendship with Rafael Caro Quintero, who is in prison in Mexico City, charged with ordering the torture and murder of DEA agent Enrique Camarena Salazar in Guadalajara in February 1986. At the time we talked, she had just received an invitation to Quintero's birthday party to be held inside Mexico City's Northern Prison. She answered the invitation, telling him that she couldn't make it because she couldn't afford the trip. A return wire advised that Caro Quintero's private jet would be available to her at Tucson International Airport on the day of the party. Again she declined.

Emiliano sprawls on the living-room couch listening to everything we say. When our conversation lags, he speaks up.

✛ One morning, about three years ago, a young lady who used to come to our parties when I was in the business staggered into my house. She was totally strung out on drugs, and I was afraid she might have overdosed. Somehow I managed to get her into my car and drove straight to my mother's house. I had to carry the girl inside; by now she couldn't walk. I was holding her under her arms, she was totally limp, her head hung to one side. I asked my mother to help her. My mother prayed to the Virgin Mary, I had never seen her this intense, the veins on her forehead stood out. She opened her eyes and put her arms around the girl.

I lost track of time, but it seemed like just a few seconds before the girl opened her eyes and was able to stand on her own two feet.

My mother was exhausted and had to sit down at the dining-room table. The girl didn't remember coming to my house or anything that happened. We didn't try to explain it to her and I took her back to my house because my mother couldn't even talk—she was so tired. On the way home the girl told me she had been shooting cocaine, she still had a high but felt better than she had in years. About an hour after we arrived at my house the phone rang. It was my mother. She was talking so fast I could barely understand what she was saying. She told me to come to her house, that she needed help. When I arrived, she was in the kitchen mopping the floor and cleaning the walls, almost at the same time. She just couldn't stop. I finally calmed her down, and she was able to lie down on the bed.

The only way we could explain the events of that morning was that she had been able to draw enough of the cocaine from the young woman's body into her own to counteract the overdose, but in doing so she had gotten a high just as if she had taken some on her own. It took her two days to come down from her high and get back to normal, but she saved the girl's life. This is one of the powers I have seen her use. ✤

Not until the fifth or sixth visit can I convince Carranza to say anything about his start in drugs. He speaks so softly the tape recorder can barely pick it up.

It is 1976. Emiliano is having trouble; he is working hard to remodel the Fremont House on South Main Street behind the Tucson Community Center, the house where John C. Fremont, a late-nineteenth-century governor of Arizona Territory, supposedly lived. Emiliano is being paid only five dollars an hour by the architect. Using his ingenuity, Emiliano is able to pad the payroll with non-existent workers from Mexico and then do the work himself.

It is about this time that Emiliano decides to buy a little burned-out Chinese grocery store where he wants to build the house of his dreams. The first thing to do is to raze the building and start from scratch.

The Fremont project is about over, leaving him out of work, and heart problems, IRS problems, not to mention a new marriage, are closing in on Emiliano. A friend offers a solution. It comes in the form of introductions to important people in Mexico who are deeply involved in the distribution of cocaine and marijuana. Through this friend he meets Ernesto and Geraldo, who own a fabulous hacienda near Caborca in Sonora. A few trial runs that Emiliano finds to be amazingly easy to complete, and then more involvement. The money is so good it's hard to turn down any of the shipments they offer him.

At first it's just marijuana shipments without any contact with the buyer—just pick up a car in Mexico, cross the border at Sasabe or Naco, deliver it to a supermarket parking lot in Tucson. Walk a few steps, pick up another car with the money inside, and head back through Nogales into Mexico.

Emiliano is a quick study and before long he is introduced to the big man himself. He knows him only as Ernesto. Last names are not important. After a few test runs he is turned over to Ernesto's partner, Geraldo, who will be Emiliano's contact from this day forth. "My advice to you is not to soil your own yard. Don't do any business in Tucson if you can avoid it. I'll give you some names in Miami, Las Vegas, and Los Angeles, and the proper way to make your contacts. Then it's up to you," Geraldo tells him.

Another week passes before Carranza is willing to talk about drugs again, and then he remembers the early days, his internship, so to speak.

✦ It started during the summer of 1976. That was when I made my first contact in Las Vegas and landed my first big contract. I was staying at one of the big hotels on the strip when the knock came on my door. I opened the door because in those days I had nothing to fear. All we were going to do was talk anyway. I did have a sample, but there wasn't that much difficulty with the law back then. I could tell right away that the visitor was Cuban or Puerto Rican by the way he spoke Spanish and the way he dressed. Very casual, with baggy cream-colored slacks and a black silk shirt with long sleeves. It was open in front, and he was wearing some fine gold chains. I have a feeling for these things and I knew immediately that this wasn't the main man.

There were three women with him, beautiful, showgirl-quality women, and I remember one of them was a black girl with huge breasts and a tight ass. I mean she didn't jiggle at all when she walked. The room was not just a room, I think they call it a suite, and it had a full bar, not the kind you have to put money in or have it charged to your room every time you remove one of those small bottles. When I am working, I don't drink, do coke, or smoke weed, but my first rule is not to become involved with the women. That's the first thing they throw at you, and let me tell you some of that pussy is damn hard to turn down sometimes.

So we do the small talk and finally he wants to see a picture. That means he wants to see what I have with me, what quality and how much. He keeps throwing the women at me, has them touching me and doing things to tempt me. Finally I got tired and told him to fuck off. He wasn't going to see my picture because he wasn't the man I wanted to talk to. He gives me the pissed-off routine and tries to scare me with a cheap-looking stiletto switchblade he uses to clean his nails.

Fifteen minutes later the doorbell rings and the first guy holds the door for his twin. Same slacks, shoes without socks, lots of gold, but this guy is for real. You can tell by the way he moves, the way he acts. No bullshit, no fancy whores, and his eyes are smart. We shake hands, talk, and I know it's all right. No small talk. I bring out my picture, give him a price and a delivery date I can live with. He likes the taste and we make a deal. Fifty pounds of cocaine delivered in two weeks. How and where is my business, he doesn't want to know. Now the first guy does his job. He will be the contact and deliver the money. Business is over, now is the time for a drink, a little coke, and the girls. ✤

Bits and pieces, that's all I get from him. Now he wants to talk about the house again, so I get a little pissed off and ask him about the wildcat. And what about the bodies in the cellar? He laughs.

✤ Go ahead and check the house, see if you can find a wildcat or even a tame cat anywhere. People are jealous of me, but they have too much respect for me to say anything to my face. I never use violence, the handguns and rifles the police took away from my house when they arrested me were for my own protection and for my pleasure. I was born on a ranch and lived in the *monte*, or outdoors, all of my early years. We were very poor and I was the best shot with a rifle, so I was the hunter for the family. As for the bodies, that is silly.

When I bought this land, it belonged to a Chinaman named Ray. The property had a small market on it right about where my cellar is now, about the middle of the house. I hired some men to tear down the store and level the ground for me so I could put in my foundation. When they were tearing up the wood floors, they came upon an iron door under the floor leading down to a cellar. I didn't know it was there. They managed to open it and the first thing that greeted them was a skeleton. The two workers were from Mexico and very superstitious, and they took off running, leaving their tools and lunch buckets behind them.

I never did get those two men to come back to work, but that's where the story about the bodies in the basement came from. The skeleton was probably a relative of Ray's who was not legal, and so when he died, Ray just buried him in the cellar. It happened a lot in the old days. You know how people make a story bigger to make it sound good.

I wanted this land because from here I can see the underpass two blocks away where I slept when I first came to Tucson from Texas. I stayed with my uncle about a week before his wife tired of feeding another mouth and kicked me out. So I slept under the bridge on South Tenth Avenue and went to the stores to steal food to eat. I was only fourteen, couldn't speak English, couldn't read or write, and couldn't find a job. A boy I had never met, who was from the Barrio Libre, saw me under the bridge looking dirty, tired, and hungry, so he took me home with him and asked his mother to give me something to eat. She told me I could stay for one night to rest up and recover my strength. His name was Jimmy, and from that first night I stayed with that wonderful family for two years. I will never forget them. ✢

The next turn in my stubborn quest to know this man concerns the photo album I found on top of a bar that first day. There is another phone call and he leaves me to study his art again. The photos in the album are of the wedding to Sally, his fourth and latest wife, the lovely Sally who was arrested with him in 1984 when he was found with thirty-one pounds of cocaine, numerous rifles and handguns, and a shoebox full of one-hundred-dollar bills. Sally and two workers who slept in the guest house were finally released and eventually the charges were dropped. Before I can slam the album shut he enters the room. He doesn't seem angry and we start looking at the wedding pictures.

✢ The wedding and the reception were at the Holidrome, but I don't really believe in weddings according to church and law because I don't believe in the church and I don't think a civil judge can declare me married. What I did was hire a Rolls-Royce limousine to drive us out to Sahuarita south of town, and we walked behind a bar out there and I carved our initials in a tree that has been there for one hundred years or more, and I myself declared Sally and Emiliano married for life.

It was funny, we were driving back to the Holidrome, and the driver is already scared because he is on the south side of town where the drug dealers and thieves live, and he thinks I am one too. I was into my macho time of life and I was going to play a joke on Sally to show her what a big man I was. I took out my revolver and placed it next to her pretty head. The driver happened to look in the mirror and saw what I was doing. He screamed, pulled to the shoulder of the road, and took off running down the middle of Twelfth Avenue. It took us half an hour to find him and a fifty-dollar tip to get him to take us the rest of the way. ✚

One of the members of the wedding is a tall, handsome Latino with straight, slicked-back hair, wearing a white suit, a white silk shirt, and a beautiful redheaded woman on his arm. She wears only one diamond necklace around her milk-white throat, but it looks very expensive. This, Emiliano tells me, is Rene, the most important man in Miami. He has come to be best man at the wedding. It's hard to explain the degree of honor he has paid Emiliano because we can't comprehend how much face is involved here, how important this would be to the career of someone aspiring to break into the big time in the drug world. It's the difference between dealing in ounces and pounds—and maybe in tons of cocaine later.

Another picture in the album grabs my attention. It's a tall Anglo with a thick moustache, wide shoulders and long hair, cowboy style. He wears an expensive cowboy suit and boots. He looks familiar, looks like a former deputy sheriff from Pima County who was asked to resign after beating to death a small-time marijuana dealer who made the mistake of shooting up the deputy's trailer and not killing him. The word on the street is that he now works as a contract hit man for some of the top drug people in Miami and Chicago. He lives up north now, up in the hills, but flies in and out of Tucson quite often. Sometimes he makes trips into Mexico. I have heard him speak of Mexican generals, *comandantes*, and government officials as if they were just guys he met in a bar.

Officers from the Department of Public Safety, the Tucson Police Department, the Pima County Sheriff's task force, and the Drug Enforcement Agency worked for eight years to get Emiliano Carranza, and by their own admission could not get near him because he was so well organized and insulated by loyal workers. In the end it was a call to 88-Crime by Emiliano's former wife, the woman with dark powers, at least in Emiliano's estimation.

Of course, Emiliano knows who turned him in, but he is carrying a five-year tail (probation) behind him and can't say or do too much, even if he wanted to.

✦ If they had come half an hour later they wouldn't have found anything, but there was an unavoidable delay in our operation, and that was enough time for them to get their warrants and find the cocaine in the guest house. Sally didn't know what was going on, so they didn't have anything on her and they released her. You have no idea how much the arrest cost me in money and what damage it did to my health. Some people say I faked a heart attack when I was busted, but they are wrong. The money came easily and left the same way.

They made too many mistakes when they arrested me, and they finally offered me five years' probation on a plea bargain. The police claimed they found thirty-one pounds of cocaine in my house, but when it came time to go to court, they could only produce one pound. Too many mistakes, but I still lost my ass. ✦

The Godfather has fallen, but his organization remains. It probably never stopped operations for more than a day or two. Another Godfather stepped right in, and the beat goes on. Rumors are that now, with Emiliano's tail almost gone, the Godfather is putting out feelers to get back in. He denies it, of course, and I heard that the Godfather was out for good and wouldn't be let back in. But the rumors also said he had a wildcat and bodies in the cellar and I didn't ever see them. If it were me, I wouldn't count him out.

2 NIGGIE'S WORLD

I felt as if I didn't have any flesh, like a
skeleton. I tried to pinch my skin but couldn't
find any. I was all bones. It was the best high
I'd ever had.

—Niggie

THE HORROR THAT WAS WORLD War II was behind us; all that was left was a need to go on to better things. New opportunities never before imagined were now available to Americans. The GI Bill and the Federal Housing Administration regulations suddenly allowed Americans from all walks of life to at least be eligible for a good education and a home of their own. This was especially beneficial to the young barrio and ghetto dwellers across the United States, who previously had little or no hope to escape their poverty.

The new peace and prosperity had not come without a price tag. The war had created a number of users addicted to heavy drugs like opium and morphine. Added to this were the remnants of the *pachuco* movement of the war years, the original drop-outs from the West Coast who created a new style of dress and a language based on slang words in their crudest form. They were the instigators of gang warfare and the first organized group to promote the sale of drugs among Mexican American communities throughout the country.

While all of the credit can't be given to a few *pachucos* wearing drapes, double-soled shoes, and long chains, they did increase the demand for drugs significantly, and their styled behavior was picked up in the ghettos of the East Coast in varying degrees but with the same ulterior motive—greed. The end result was the same all over: increased drug use and a rise of crimes such as burglary, armed robbery, and the most popular crime of the addict, shoplifting.

The increase in the popularity of drugs in the early 1950s was spreading from New York to Seattle and was already coming to the attention of law enforcement officials all over the country, even though they were slow to respond. Change was hard to come by in the prewar years, and the postwar era wasn't any different.

In general, police agencies were convinced it was just another craze that would soon disappear with the "chucos" and their fancy clothes.

♦ ♦ ♦

Niggie and I were raised in the same barrio in downtown Tucson. Our paths crossed many times, as with most people in Tucson during the 1930s and 1940s. We were never really friends until much later in life. He ran with a different crowd. Niggie and his friends were always on the other side of the law, guys you could get a bad reputation from. They seldom went to school, hardly ever worked, always had money, and were always looking for trouble. They were the ones who picked fights after school or after the football games. Girls who hung out with or dated Niggie and his friends were automatically considered whores. They were the wild bunch, the *rascuachos* (a slang term we used to describe low-life bums), *ladrones* (thieves), and *malcriados*, those who are ill-bred and have no respect. It came as no surprise when Niggie was sent to Ft. Grant, the juvenile detention center.

I lived at the edge of the barrio, and my friends were more into sports, going to movies, and we went to school pretty regularly. We did our homework while listening to Jack Benny or Fibber Magee and Molly on the radio. Niggie and his bunch worked at being cool, hip characters who crowded people off the sidewalk when they walked our version of cruising the drag. We walked the drag because most of us didn't even have bicycles, much less low-riders. Niggie's friends enjoyed breaking into lockers and disrupting the social hour every Friday afternoon in the basement of the school. They were the first to smoke, to drink, to get a girl in trouble, to try pot, and the first to go to jail.

Niggie and his friends went their way and we went ours. But we were all from the barrio, and there is a kind of bond that makes us all friends. Niggie went to jail and I became a cop. Our adult paths didn't cross very often because he was in jail much of the seven years I worked on the narcotics detail in Tucson. I have a feeling that Niggie and the other *rascuachos* of the barrios were probably not any worse than some of the kids you knew in your hometown when you were growing up, but they did form the nucleus of a drug network that exists in Tucson and the Southwest to this day. They provided the stepping-stones for the likes of Jaime Figueroa Soto and his Mexican counterparts to create a hub-city for the distribution of marijuana, heroin, and later cocaine to the far corners of this country. It was Niggie's friends who went to Mexico to buy drugs and made the contacts with the *cholos* (low-class Mexicans) from the slums of Sonora. Later these Mexican drug dealers would become known as mafiosos because the Mexican people likened them to the Italian Mafia.

The *cholos* embraced the name. It gave them new power and a feeling of respect, even if it was respect created by fear. In retrospect we didn't take them seriously enough at first. They came to Tucson with four or five sets of identification and funny sounding names, and it was hard to remember that they also used their mother's name at the end. They came to Tucson and gave new meaning to the term "safe house," and because of these *cholo* mafiosos new expressions became household words, like money laundering and cocaine corridor.

✤ I think we were the poorest in a neighborhood where hard times was a way of life. I was eight years old before I had my first pair of shoes. They were hand-me-downs and already had holes. I was in the second grade when Mrs. Maldonado showed my dirty feet to the class. She held me up by the ankles, and I admit they were really filthy. There was a pretty girl in class who kind of liked me. After that she refused to talk to me. On the way home from school that day I made up my mind never to be hungry or dirty again. In the winter I heated water and bathed in a large tin tub, in the summer I used the irrigation ditch west of town.

The barrio where I was born and lived for so many years, when I wasn't in jail or in the Army, was called the Barrio Libre. It had a tough reputation from the early days when Tucson was still mostly Mexican. When I was growing up, it had tamed down a lot, but we still had the whorehouses in Sabino Alley and bars that stayed open after hours and places where the men could go gamble without too much interference from the police. I was kind of wild, and after my mother died my dad couldn't control me. I went where I wanted and did whatever pleased me. I can't really blame the barrio or my parents or anyone for what happened to me, but I suspect that if I had been born on the other side of town and my skin were white instead of deep brown, and if my father had been a businessman or doctor instead of a part-time brick layer and *curandero* [healer], things might be different for me. But I'm not complaining. I have had some damn good times in my life, I've had money, women, cars, everything people today judge your success by. I didn't have those things for long, but I had them. There were other guys in the barrio that were as bad off as I was, but they pulled through, they went to school, got good jobs, and made a good life.

Hey, I know the drug scene. I have been using drugs of one kind or another for forty-five years. People always ask me how I got hooked. I tell the social workers what they want to hear, that I started the way most addicts do, using a little marijuana, then experimenting with opium, and finally getting hooked on heroin. I'm the first to admit that I was a criminal in the sense that I have committed numerous crimes in order to maintain my habit. Hey *ese*, I loved heroin. When you fix on heroin it's like being with a woman, it gives you great pleasure and sometimes a lot of grief. When I got that rush of the drug going through my veins, it was like a climax with my favorite lady, only better, and it lasted longer.

In 1943 I was fourteen and fresh out of Ft. Grant reform school. They said I was incorrigible because I ditched a lot of school and got caught stealing from the stores and a couple of houses, small stuff like that. Reform school wasn't half-bad. I found out that I have a tolerance for being locked up. A lot of guys go crazy doing time because they let it fuck up their minds, they worry too much about the long term, they don't do one day at a time like you're supposed to. Anyway, I was free and living at home, but as usual I was able to roam free. These were exciting times. World War II was in full swing, the entire country was booming, and there were so many ways to make money. In reform school I learned about drugs without actually trying them. What I mean is I could see the guys using pills and marijuana and shit like that, but I just didn't feel like doing it. They dared me, called me a pussy, *ratta* [informer], and things like that, but I don't care what people say about me as long as I know it isn't true.

I remember very well the first time I did marijuana. It was a warm summer afternoon right after I was released from Ft. Grant. I walked to town to catch a movie or whatever form of entertainment presented itself. I didn't have any money, but that wasn't a problem. If I couldn't bum a quarter from someone I could always sneak in.

In those days Congress Street in downtown Tucson divided itself into two parts: to the east of Stone Avenue were the banks, department stores, the better shops, bars, restaurants, and theaters; to the west of Stone it became a Mexican town, or actually an extension of the barrio. The bars, restaurants, barber shops, pawn shops, and clothing stores all catered to a Mexican clientele. In the middle of a

long block as the street started curving down to the west, there was a
bar called La Selva, a basement nightclub owned and operated by
the Alianza Hispana Americana, a fraternal organization dedicated
to the impossible task of social and political unity for Mexican
Americans.

I stopped in the entryway to La Selva to hear the music coming
from below. La Selva means "The Jungle" and I found out later that it
was well named. It was a *tardeada*, or afternoon dance. A poster on
the wall advertised the music of Uchi Hernandez, and at the bottom
it said there was going to be *cahuama* [Mexican soup made from
giant sea turtles] served. I remember I was wearing my black drapes
[baggy pants that taper down to a narrow cuff at the ankles], a white
T-shirt, and my good double-soled cordovan wingtips that I polished
with ox-blood shine. I was leaning on the wall in the hall when two
guys I knew from the barrio who were on leave from the Army came
up for air. I asked them for a quarter for the movies, but instead they
offered me some marijuana. I was in the mood for something different so I accepted.

We walked west on Congress away from town. It wasn't until after
we passed the tracks behind the Southern Pacific Hospital that they
lit up. I know now that it was really good weed, the purple marijuana
from Mexico. It was a little sticky, like the gum on the mesquite
pods. I confessed to them I had never done pot before but wanted to
try it. They could tell I was scared and they laughed, but eventually
they showed me how to draw the smoke deeply into my lungs and
hold it. At first I was disappointed, I didn't feel anything. It tasted
sweet and smelled good, but no different from smoking a Camel. We
smoked maybe two or three joints and were walking back toward
town, and I was about to tell them I didn't feel anything from their
chicken-shit marijuana, when it hit me. The high was so good I don't
remember walking back to town. I felt as if I didn't have any flesh,
like a skeleton. I tried to pinch my skin but couldn't find any. I was
all bones. It was the best high I'd ever had. I don't think I've ever

had better. But it was my first time and I guess it's like the first woman you sleep with . . . you never forget it.

I ran around with Peewa Jaurequi, Mickey Molina, Speedy, and Chonito. There wasn't anything we wouldn't try. All of us had been to Ft. Grant at one time or the other and this formed a sort of bond. We were walking toward town one Saturday afternoon to see if we could roll some drunk Indians or maybe sell a few joints of marijuana to the pool shooters in the back of the Legal Tender Saloon. Near Sabino Alley, where the whores lived, we met Fernando Moncada, a guy much older than we were. We knew he used opium and was a drug dealer. Moncada was tall and thin, in his early forties, and had a badly broken nose. Right out front he asked us if we wanted to fix up some opium. Scared the shit out of me, but I didn't want to punk out on the guys, so I went along with them. I figured I could fake it and get away as soon as they started to nod out.

From the backyard of his house near Sabino Alley Moncada brought in a bag with some stuff that looked like paving tar. There was also an eyedropper with a hypodermic needle attached, some cotton, and a spoon with the handle bent backward so that it stood on its own. The spoon was blackened by the countless matches or candles used to heat the opium until it boiled. Moncada added a little water and cooked up some opium. They took turns fixing. Finally it was my turn and Moncada asked me if I wanted to try it. When he saw me hesitate, he told me to at least try fixing the cottons. I didn't want to, but everyone was looking at me, waiting to see if I would chicken out. I finally agreed, not knowing that the best part of the opium was in the residue left in the cottons.

He did everything for me. He put the belt around my arm as a tourniquet and slipped the needle into the big vein in my right arm. I still remember the sensation. It hit me like a bolt of lightning as soon as he released it into my vein. Even before he pulled the needle out, I was already fucked up. I remember that my toes curled up inside my shoes. I could feel them curl up, but there wasn't anything I could do about it. Then a wonderful warm feeling came over me. Then I wanted to throw up. Opium does that to you at first. Moncada noticed it. He told me to go outside. Shit, I couldn't even get up, how did he expect me to go outside? He laughed at me and helped me out. I must have thrown up a hundred times.

Despite the fear and the nausea I loved the feeling of euphoria that came after the first jolt. Moncada kept on giving us as much opium as we wanted until he was sure we were hooked. Then he cut us off. I was still just chipping around, just sticking my arm for the kicks once in a while, because every time I smell opium or heroin cooking I get sick to my stomach. In order to fix I had to go outside while someone prepared the eyedropper and then wait until everyone had fixed before I came back. That's why I seldom fixed alone and was vulnerable to snitches or anyone who wanted to get even with me. You never know who is going to give you up or load up a hot shot so you can overdose. In those days we didn't have to worry about AIDS or anything like that. We always fixed with the same needle, six or seven guys at a time. A couple of guys got hepatitis because they used dirty needles or got some dirty dope.

It was much easier when I first started doing dope seriously because law enforcement, as far as narcotics was concerned, was lax. Most of the young men from Tucson had gone to war and the police were very shorthanded. Really, the only cop we had to worry about was a big guy by the name of Joe "Brownie" Brown, a motor-cycle officer. Brownie was the only one who had any idea of what was coming down in narcotics and who was doing what. Once in a long while Brownie would hassle us and take away our joints or bust our outfits for fixing, but it was a halfhearted effort.

We learned right away that we could make a better deal in Nogales, Sonora, so we went there instead of buying from Moncada. It was so easy crossing the border with drugs that at first I thought it was legal. Most of the time we just carried it in our pockets or hidden in our socks. Usually the border guards never even got up

from the chair they were sitting on. They would ask you if you were
carrying any liquor or fruit and where you were born. They never
asked about drugs, so I never lied to them. When they did check, it
was to see if you were trying to smuggle in things that were rationed
or parrots.

My favorite place to hang out was Jimmy's Chicken Shack on
Meyer Street, the hottest nightclub in town during the middle forties
and early fifties. A favorite of the after-hours crowd, mostly white,
street-wise people. At Jimmy's you could find hookers, gamblers,
con men, and thieves rubbing elbows with businessmen, doctors,
lawyers, and the new wave of upbeat college students, all looking for
a few thrills. Oddly enough, very few black people ever went to the
Shack. Jimmy Mitchell, the owner, was a tall, stocky black dude
with light olive skin. He wasn't fat, just heavy-set. Jimmy had jet-
black wavy hair, which he wore long and well greased. He was also a
pimp and marijuana dealer. He never used any dope but marijuana.
He loved marijuana. Jimmy wore pin-striped, double-breasted
suits and sharp-pointed patent leather shoes with thin soles and
high heels.

Across the street from the Chicken Shack was a small shoeshine
parlor where we hung out. They had a juke box and a back room
where we could smoke pot or fix up if we wanted to. It was more of a
gathering place than a clubhouse because the membership was open
and constantly changing. Come to think of it, there weren't any
formal gangs with fancy names like you hear about now. When there
was trouble, it was one barrio against the other. Even the *pachucos*
from Los Angeles could never really get established here. They were
more or less forced out by the servicemen who kicked their ass in
one great battle after another in downtown L.A. during the riots of
1942. After that the *pachucos* spread out into Arizona, Colorado,
New Mexico, and Texas, trying to keep their movement alive.

Jimmy Mitchell was pretty careful about who he allowed in the
Chicken Shack. Troublemakers were roughly handled by three burly
bouncers, and minors were not allowed. Most of the women in his

string were white, even though he did have a few black whores working for him. A few of us were allowed to hang around the joint because Jimmy came to depend on us to supply him with marijuana. There were a few rooms in back where the hookers took the customers, and I remember a small courtyard where Jimmy sold marijuana.

In those wartime years and through the early fifties, the railroad was the most popular form of transportation, and very often dance bands going through stopped in Tucson for a few hours or a few days. Name bands too, not just the ham-and-eggers, and they all knew about Jimmy's Chicken Shack. When they had a layover in Tucson, they always wound up jamming at Jimmy's. One of my personal favorites was the Illinois Jazz Cats. The leader of the band played the meanest, sweetest saxophone in the world. I would sit next to the small stage in back and feed him joints so he would keep playing. Sometimes the jam sessions would go well into the morning. The cops seldom bothered Jimmy, but if they did, he just paid a fine and was back in business.

During the week we took the bus to Nogales to buy a couple of pounds of marijuana for Jimmy. We paid forty bucks for two pounds and sold them to Jimmy for eighty. To show you how easy it was, we simply put the marijuana into two or three shopping bags, the kind that have handles, and just mixed it in with packages of candy and cheap curios we bought in Nogales. Then we separated and just walked across the border and met at the bus stop.

Before the weekend arrived, Jimmy hired two or three of us to roll marijuana cigarettes at his house for a penny a joint. We sat around a table in the front room rolling joints on a large piece of canvas that covered the entire table. We would roll one and steal one. One morning we really had rolled a lot of joints and had our pockets full of marijuana. Shit, the room smelled like there was field of marijuana on fire and we were really getting stoned. There was a knock on the door. Jimmy was in the bedroom sleeping, so his wife went to see who it was.

The next thing I knew, his old lady was screaming that it was the cops and Jimmy was running around naked, his balls banging on his knees, and he was going crazy. She was screaming, we were laughing hysterically. Jimmy snatched the canvas off the table and ran to the bathroom to flush the marijuana. She kept screaming for us to go out the back way and Jimmy kept flushing the toilet. It finally dawned on us that we could go to jail, so we jumped up to leave. It was a scene from the Keystone Kops. We all hit the back door and bounced back because we all tried to get out at the same time. I remember windows flying open and, despite ourselves, we all made it out into the backyard and scattered. When we saw Jimmy the next day, he was furious. All the cops wanted was to ask about a citation that he'd already paid. He even tried to put the blame on us for losing two pounds of marijuana and stopping up the toilet. We laughed at him and made another trip to Nogales.

There were always plenty of customers for marijuana and I always kept a pretty good stash. When I was short of money or wanted to fix up some opium, I rolled some joints and sold them in the barrio or in the bars on Congress Street.

In 1946 I had just got out of jail for shoplifting and decided to join the Army and see what the world was like away from the barrio and prison. Much to my surprise I passed all of the tests and was sworn in. After boot camp I was assigned to the medical corps and became, of all things, a medic. Talk about leaving the wolf to watch the sheep.

After corps school in California, I was assigned to Fitzsimmon Army Hospital in Denver, Colorado, where I went to work in the emergency room with a buddy from corps school. I soon found out we both used dope, and here we were with access to the medicine cabinets where the drugs were stored. It was easy for us to steal just enough morphine to stay high without being caught. We could always stiff the patients by giving them sugar pills or sugar water when it called for painkillers or morphine.

It didn't last long. I met this fine-looking lady in Denver at a bar where the *tecatos* [addicts] hung out, and before I knew it, we were really fixing up a lot of shit every night. I felt the noose getting tighter at the hospital and I didn't want to go to prison, so I went to see my company commander, a nice guy by the name of Jimenez, and asked for a deal. I told Captain Jimenez I was a drug addict and I knew I was going to get in trouble if he didn't find a way to get me out early. Captain Jimenez agreed to do what he could. The Army was gearing for peacetime and it was easy to get out. They actually wanted people to get out. A few days later they offered me a general discharge under honorable conditions. I grabbed at the deal and within a month I was on my way home. Two months later the Korean War started and I was on my way to prison again. I was arrested for possession of narcotics on my way out of Colorado.

I was arrested in 1963 for a string of burglaries, robberies, and if convicted, I would be a four-time loser. I knew I was looking at a mandatory life sentence without parole. The detectives from the Sheriff's Department wanted me to snitch on someone they wanted real bad.

I had been caught in Phoenix, and when they were bringing me back, one of the detectives sat next to me. I had known him since we were both kids. He's a big bastard and doesn't have a kind bone in his body. When I refused to set up this guy for him or tell him anything I knew, he started working on my ribs, punching me hard and smiling at me. I don't know, I was looking at life. But shit, he was a bigger crook than I was. Why should I help him out? I took it, and later I managed to have my lawyer talk to the county attorney and remand me back to Phoenix where they also had some felony charges against me. Then I got lucky. The county attorney in Phoenix failed to file any prior convictions on me. I couldn't get to court fast enough to plead guilty.

The judge was a woman. She wanted to throw the book at me, but since they hadn't filed priors there wasn't anything she could do about it. She chewed my ass out and sentenced me to the max, three to five years. In all the time I was in prison I was always under the gun, never made trusty or stepped outside of the walls. When I was released in 1966 after doing my three years, I went right back to the barrio. This time I wasn't going back to the joint. I made myself that promise.

What really made me stop using dope was that I got tired. My father died when I was in the joint. I remember going back to my cell after they told me. I was feeling sorry for myself, mad at the whole world because I wasn't there when he died. Even if we didn't get along because I was so bad, I always had a pact with him and I prayed for him at night when I went to bed. One of the guards asked me what was the matter and I snapped at him that it wasn't any of his business. He was patient with me, and finally I told him what had happened, and he asked if I wanted him to talk to the warden so they would let me go to the funeral. I refused. Fuck no, I didn't want any favors. He gave me the rest of the day off from my job. That night I cried.

The next morning this same guard asked me what I was going to do. I told him the funeral was the next day and there wouldn't be time. He looked at me for some time and then he told me, "If you don't go see your dad, the gates are going to close behind your ass for the rest of your life." He was an old German, even had the accent. Nobody liked him because he was real strict and always went by the book, but he arranged for me to go to the funeral.

After that I just got tired of doing time, seeing all of the killings, the things that happen to men behind bars, the rapes, beatings, extortion, robbery, human beings becoming animals. I was going to see the yard captain for something I needed one morning. I had just walked out and right there in front of me was a black guy just standing in line. This dude came out of the yard and started whacking at his head with a pipe. I can still hear the sound of the pipe hitting the poor guy's skull, like the thump from a watermelon bursting open.

There was a guy from Tucson, Mendoza, who at one time was a

pretty big dealer before he got busted and started snitching for Marmion and Dunn [Tucson cops]. The man had a hell of a jacket [reputation] on him when he finally got busted and sent back to the joint. You see, when the cops have a snitch, he's got to stay clean and not pull any shit on his own. He can't be pulling burglaries and selling dope on his own and that's what Mendoza had been doing.

I was in the yard one day when two guys cornered him and were going to kill him for what he was or what they thought he was. Mendoza stood right up to them and never begged or backed down an inch. I remember he told them: "Go ahead and kill me, I'm not worth anything, you're not going to kill anything, and then what's going to happen to you guys? You're going to stay here longer than I will. Go ahead, kill me." He was just talking shit because that's all he could do, but they bought it and left him alone.

The kind of killings I've seen in prison are savage. It scared the shit out of me. I had always done easy time in my head, but I had seen too much. In prison there's no place to run. Where can you run? You have to come out of that cell sometime, and those people have a lot of time, they wait real good. Even if you didn't owe anyone anything, you had to be careful. You could walk around a corner and someone could hit you with a shank or a lead pipe just because he didn't like you, or for no reason at all. That's what scared me. There's a lot of crazy people on the inside. I said, no more, no more using heroin, no more time. All of the time I was in prison I had all of the heroin or any kind of drug I wanted, any time I wanted some, and had the money or power to get it.

There are a lot of ways to bring drugs into the joint—crooked guards, family, girlfriends, and wives passing it to you, but the one I enjoyed watching the most was the way Camachito brought it in. Camachito was a lifer who had been in the joint since the 1930s for killing his partner by hitting him with a pick in the back. They were smuggling mescal and tequila in from Mexico and had been hiding the money in the desert. One night Camachito caught his partner digging up the stash and killed him. When I met him, it was 1963, on my last bust, and he was a trusty living in a shack outside the walls with about a hundred cats. He was a likable old man who got along with everyone. He made his money in a lot of ways, but his main source of income was smuggling in marijuana.

Camachito was in charge of the trash detail. They had an old horse-drawn wagon that came inside the walls and hauled off the garbage cans, replacing the filled cans with shiny new empty ones. But the new cans weren't always empty, Camachito would tape packages of marijuana to the bottom or on the underside of the lids, and his inside contacts would pick them up. Eventually someone must have ratted because one morning they busted him and the warden brought him inside the walls for ninety days. Then they let him go back to his shack.

After I got out, the new cops didn't know who I was and life in the barrio was pretty good. I met a nice lady. We were married in 1968, and I settled down to a happy life. I found a job as a bartender. I had done my time and wasn't on parole or anything like that, so I could work where I wanted. We were able to get a pretty nice apartment in the government housing project known as La Reforma. She had four young children of her own and soon we had a new baby girl. It was the only good thing I had ever done in my life. This was all new to me. I had never had anyone dependent on me before. I had never supported anything but my habit. It was tough making it on a bartender's salary even though I tapped the till from time to time like any good bartender will.

The godfather of our child was deeply involved in the smuggling and sale of heroin and cocaine. He became my *compadre*, and this obligated both of us to help each other and our families out whenever it was needed. My *compadre* was doing very well, he had a new house, several cars, a boat, and in his refrigerator there was a milk carton in the freezer section with thirty thousand in cash. We needed money, so he offered me a deal to bring stuff over for him. My *compadre* provided us with a car and he paid me between two and four hundred dollars, depending on how much I brought back for him.

My wife loved the trips to Nogales, especially when I insisted we

take the kids. She didn't even care when I left her at the Fray
Marcos hotel with the children while I went to have a drink across
the street at a bar that was well known as a meeting place for drug
transactions. It was in front of this bar that the best-known drug
dealer in Nogales, Sonora, parked his taxicab. His name was Pancho
Ortega, but everyone called him "Santanon." He was a big guy who
towered up over six feet when he wore his cowboy boots.

Before I left my wife I always gave her plenty of money to shop at
the stores. She thought I was wonderful to take her shopping in
Nogales with her children. I must tell you that my wife never had
any idea what I was doing. If she had, she would have died right
there. I usually brought close to a pound or more of heroin wrapped
around my body. When we crossed the border, we looked like any
other couple doing a little shopping with their children. The customs
agents never bothered us. Who would suspect a man with five kids
and a wife who was so obviously straight? They waved us through
without even checking the car.

Like I said, my *compadre* paid me damn good money, and with
what I was knocking down at the bar we were living pretty well. We
were partying almost every night and both of us were drinking quite
a bit. But I wasn't fixing up. Well, maybe once in a while I would
chip around with the guys, but I had it under control.

We lasted together much longer than most expected, much longer
than I thought I could stay straight. The action was getting heavier in
the barrio and it was getting harder and harder to stay straight. Then
she got religious and didn't want me to smoke or drink in the house.
She didn't want to party anymore and tried to convert me into a holy
roller. There were words between us, and I can't keep my mouth
shut, so we had some nasty scenes in front of the kids that I
regretted later. Finally I moved out and went to stay with Mickey
Molina and his old lady. Mickey and I go back a long way in the
barrio. He was my best friend, a guy you could trust. We shared a lot
of needles together.

When things go bad, they can really turn sour. I lost my job at the bar because the boss said I was drinking on duty and wasn't being careful enough with the register. Shit, man, how careful can you get? I knew every penny I took from him. Then George came to stay with Mickey for a few days. I never did trust the bastard and I knew he was strung out on heroin.

George knew about a sure thing, a house burglary with nothing but the best goods. I didn't like it, but I finally agreed to be the driver for Mickey to help him out. But I told them I was going to stay two blocks away until they gave me a signal that they were ready. Then I would drive up and they could load the merchandise. I also told them that if I saw any heat or even suspected anything, I was going to get the hell out of there and they would be on their own. The operation went off without a hitch. We brought the shit back to Mickey's house and celebrated our good fortune. It was all good stuff and there was even a gun among the goods.

The next day Mickey told us he was going out to sell the gun. I offered to drive him, but Mickey wanted to go alone. We had been drinking all night and well into the morning and we even did a little heroin, so I didn't argue with him. A short time later I heard George leave the house. When Mickey didn't come home after two or three hours, his old lady Betty and I started to get worried. It doesn't take very long to sell a gun in this town, so I figured he was out trying to get some more heroin. The last time anyone had seen Mickey, he was in front of the Shamrock Bar on South Sixth Avenue. He was seen getting into a car with George's brother Johnny and some other *tecatos*. I couldn't find him anywhere so I went back to the house.

Later in the afternoon a police officer came to notify Mickey's wife that he was dead. The officer showed us a picture of Mickey lying on the embalming table at the morgue, his eyes and mouth open. He looked shocked, surprised that he'd been unable to handle the heroin he'd ingested. After the officer left, I took Betty to notify Mickey's family and to leave her with her family. I went straight back to the house and removed all of the stolen goods we'd taken in the burglary the night before. I drove straight to Nogales and sold everything. When I came back to the house about a week later, George was waiting for me. He looked pissed and as soon as I got out of the car, he pulled a gun from under his shirt. He scared the shit out of me, but I knew I had to tough it out and not show him any fear.

"If you're not going to use that fucking gun, you better put it away and forget about it, because you're not going to get a penny after what happened to Mickey, you asshole," I told him. I walked around him and into the house. We all knew that George's brother had traded Mickey some really good heroin for the damn gun and hadn't bothered to tell him just how good it was. With Mickey drinking the way he was, the hot shot had exploded inside of him and stopped his heart. What makes it worse is that they were with him when he fixed up and watched him overdose. When they realized he was in bad shape, they took him to St. Mary's Hospital and dumped him in the parking lot. Then they called the hospital and told them where he was and what had happened. By the time they found Mickey, he was dead.

When something like this happens, it calls for retaliation; a few months later Mickey's cousins caught up with Johnny and the guys who were with Mickey when he died and made them pay dearly. When they were through with Johnny, he was crippled for life. I don't think they even bothered to dump him out in front of St. Mary's Hospital.

After the old lady and I broke up I still wanted to see my daughter and even her kids, but it just didn't work out. I was still working for my *compadre* but mostly in town. I was more or less a runner for him, picking up money from his wholesale customers. He gave me a new car and a gun because I was picking up a lot of money, sometimes ten or twenty thousand a night.

Smuggling dope was nothing new to me. I've done it hundreds of times. Once, in 1956, I went to Nogales with a tall, good-looking black pimp and one of his ladies who went by the name of Thelma.

We drove to the red-light district on Canal Street where he was buying his heroin at the time. While we were fixing up, the dealer loaded Thelma's cootch with heroin wrapped in condoms. Then he got some masking tape and taped her all up so the dope wouldn't fall out. When we crossed the border, Thelma was walking kind of funny, but they didn't stop us.

Another time, I think it was in 1962, the customs officers were starting to crack down on drugs at the border because of all the heat that was coming down from Washington. So we had to find other ways to bring the shit in. I made my connection in Nogales and had a guy take me to the outskirts of town. I waited until almost dark and then went to the train station on the Mexican side. I walked along the track until I found a combination freight and passenger train that I knew was headed for the American side. I had the drugs strapped to my body with tape and I crawled under a boxcar. I had some suction cups under my jacket that my connection had got for me, similar to those used to move large panes of glass. I attached them to the bottom of the car. There was a narrow platform that ran the length of the underside of the boxcar, and I lay down on it. I heard the conductor up ahead give the "all aboard" and I felt the jerk of the wheels as we rolled forward. It didn't take but a few minutes to reach the border crossing and we were in the United States. I could feel the train slow to a stop for the customs inspection. When I heard the officers coming, I pulled myself up with the suction cups and wrapped my feet around a long heavy metal bar that runs from side to side on the car.

The railroad cops and the customs inspectors flashed their lights under the cars as they went by but didn't look up under the car. Once we were across the border and picking up speed toward Tucson, I lowered myself down to the narrow platform and relaxed. The next stop was at Sahuarita, south of town, where the train stopped to pick up ore from the mines. From here it was a short walk to the Sahuarita Bar where I had a car waiting for me. From there it was a short ride into town and I was home free. But this was the hard way to do it. The best way was when my *compadre* made a connection with a trucking firm that brought watermelons and tomatoes from Mexico into Nogales, Arizona. The dock was located on the outskirts of town and I would take a taxi out there and pick up a certain car in the employee parking lot and drive it to Tucson. Once I was back in Tucson, I drove to a shopping center on the South Side. I parked the car at a designated place and picked up my own car and drove away. Another driver picked up the first car and drove it to the East Coast.

So what happened? I didn't get busted, but my *compadre* and his wife did. I was out of business again. *Gracias a dios.*

After my *compadre* went to prison, I thought very seriously about staying with the guys who took his place. The risks would be greater and I knew the odds were getting shorter for me every time I went out on a run, so I decided to go into something with more of a future. Something happened in 1982 that convinced me I had made the right decision.

I knew a young man from Agua Prieta who was living in the barrio. I'm not sure whether he was legal or not, but he had a regular job and seemed to be doing very well. I met him at the bar where I was working as a bartender. He was a hell of a nice little guy, never bothered anyone, had his beers, and then went home. Then, for some reason, he stopped coming in. When you're tending bar, you get to know your regulars, and it's only natural to ask around if they don't show up. He used to come in with this other guy who was also a wetback, or I guess now you call them "illegal aliens" or "undocumented persons." We called them *cholos.* Anyway, they stopped coming in, so I figured they had been busted by Immigration.

Then another *cholo* who sometimes came in with the little guy walks in and I asked about him. He told me that both the little guy and his friend were dead. He said they brought a camper full of top-grade marijuana across from Agua Prieta that they were supposed to deliver for this black dude at a barn in one of the cotton camps in

Marana, just north of Tucson. The black dude who hired them was in a lead car running interference, to make sure there weren't any roadblocks. They were supposed to deliver the stuff, get their money, and the guy in the car was going to bring them back to town. But there were three other black guys hiding inside the barn, waiting for them with pistols. As soon as they got out of the camper, the black guys opened fire and got all three, the two *cholos* and the black dude in the lead car. Then they threw them in the trunk of the lead car, took them out into one of the fields, and set the car on fire.

What bothers me is that they could have just tied them up. But no, they had to kill them. That's what happens now. Life is very cheap in the drug trade. It was just easier for them to kill my friend and his partners. According to the story I heard, the killers then drove the camper to New York where it was supposed to go in the first place. Marana was just the drop-off point. The police caught them in New York with part of the marijuana, but I never did find out what happened to them. But that's only one story about one delivery and sale that turned out to be a rip-off murder. It happens so often in so many different places around here that even if the cops knew about them, they couldn't ever keep up with it.

It scares the shit out of me to try anything anymore. Sure, I could be making big money, I could be having me an expensive apartment, a beautiful car, money in my pocket, and all kinds of women running in and out all the time, but I don't want to, it's not worth it. I guess I'm getting old. If God gives me another twenty years of life, that's all I want. Maybe I'll become a Jehovah's Witness.

A lady I know is looking for a husband, but he has to join her religion. If I take my Antabuse pills, then I can stop drinking for as long as I want. She said I could drink a few beers as long as I didn't drink to get drunk, but she won't live with anyone who does drugs. That's the only way I can do it. If I take my pills I can become a productive citizen. I still have a whole bunch of pills. I guess I haven't taken too many. Maybe next year.

Another thing that scares me is AIDS. I have to be very careful because I know so many people that still use the needle, and because I have my sexual needs I sometimes need favors from certain women. There was this one woman whose husband is in the joint at Wilmot Prison. She was taking care of me, if you know what I mean. I had to cut her loose because I heard that there were a lot of guys coming out of Wilmot Prison lately who are all drug addicts and friends of her husband, and they've been staying at her place. They have been shooting up in her house and, as a favor to her husband, she sleeps with them. They haven't been with a woman for a long time. She swears she hasn't been fixing with them, but who knows? She screws them and then comes to me. How do I know they don't have AIDS?

I can fix anytime I want to. I know three places right down the street, just a few houses away from here on Main Street, where I can buy heroin, marijuana, cocaine, pills, anything I want. I really don't give a damn what those people do. That's why I survive in the barrio, 'cause I mind my own business. Whatever they want to do to themselves or to one another is all right by me. The only time I would respond is if they fucked with my family. I'm not saying I don't do a little coke or some weed once in a while, and I've fixed up a few times, but I have it under control. Some of the guys I know who have been addicts for thirty or forty years are surviving now because they are on methadone. They still pick themselves with a needle from time to time, but they are able to stay out of prison because the methadone can maintain them until they make enough for a fix. They don't have that urgency to get money.

Personally I don't care for methadone, and I say this having been one of the first counselors at the Hope Center, a federal methadone program located right here in downtown Tucson. It was a couple of years after I was released from prison and still riding the rim. It was a fifty-fifty chance which way I would fall, back to prison or free on the streets. That's when President Nixon came to my rescue with his Model Cities program. I met a guy who grew up in the barrio and found out he was working for Model Cities, hiring minorities for different jobs and placing people in educational programs. He told me that the government was looking for a few good former drug addicts to train as counselors in the methadone program. We went to his office on Congress Street and he helped me fill out the application papers. He told me they would be in touch. I figured, sure you will, but I wasn't doing anything and it had helped kill some time.

A couple of months went by. I moved two or three times and forgot all about Model Cities until a friend told me that the dude from the barrio had been looking for me. I walked downtown to his office, and damned if he didn't seem glad to see me. Hired me right on the spot. We filled out more papers and I started attending classes put on by the social workers who would be running the program. One of the first things we had to do after the training period ended was to pound the streets, looking for addicts to enter into the program. Believe me, it was tough to sell these people the idea that we were going to wean them off heroin or whatever hard drug they were using and give them another drug that was even more addicting, and give it to them for the rest of their lives for nothing. All they had to do was come in every day to the Hope Center, get their fix, and piss in a bottle once a week to make sure they were clean of any other drugs.

After the program was started, they sent some of the counselors to New Mexico for a seminar. It was me and two other guys riding in one car. One of the counselors, Eddie Alacran (he's dead now, God rest his soul), was on methadone. I was driving and I asked Eddie if they had given him any methadone to take with him. They had given him a week's supply, and since I had never tried it, I thought I would, to have a better idea of what was going on. So he gave me twenty grams, two tablets of ten grams each, and when we were near St. David, Arizona, I dropped both of them. We got to Lordsburg around two in the afternoon and stopped at a restaurant to eat, and so far I didn't feel anything. We sat down to order and then bam, whoom, bam! I got that rush. The same thing as if I had fixed a heavy dose of heroin. I had to run to the bathroom to dump my guts.

Anyway, we got to Albuquerque that evening, checked in at the place we were supposed to meet, went next door to the Highway Inn where we were staying, and met a whole bunch of drug-addict counselors from all over the Southwest. Most of them were men, but there were a few fine-looking women too. I was high all that day, all night, and until the next night about eight before I got off that fucking shit. That's how good that methadone is.

Now they're making it into a liquid because some of the clients were hiding the pills under their lips or tongues or wherever and selling them on the street for forty dollars a bottle. If they were good patients, we were trusting them and giving them a bottle of pills every three days. They were selling it and buying heroin for themselves. When they knew they were going to test, they would get a sample from a relative or friend who was clean and then go into the bathroom and pour it into the sample tube. The program was new and we still had a lot of bugs to iron out.

Then there's a lot of guys like "Chuco," who takes his methadone and then goes home and gets drunk to keep that high going all day and night until he can get some more methadone the next day. I estimate that maybe one out of twenty clients is able to hold a job and be a productive citizen. I know a client who has worked for the City Maintenance Department for twenty years and faithfully goes in every morning for his fix. It's kind of sad to sit in the park across the street and watch them come to the Hope Center for their daily fix. It reminds me a little of the cows coming in from the fields to eat their oats and hay and to be milked dry so they won't have that pain.

I have moved from the barrio. I apply for every benefit that comes along through the federal, county, or city governments, and I'm on disability through the Social Security program because I hurt my back on my last job. I live in the Martin Luther King apartments for almost nothing, I get food stamps, and go get my free government cheese every Thursday. There's a lot of ways to make money legally and some not so legal.

I have a lady friend who used to take me around to all the centers that gave away the government cheese, and we would sign up for cheese and flour or beans or whatever they had that day. Then we went to the bars and restaurants on the South Side to sell the cheese for four or five bucks a pop. The flour and beans we sold in the barrio. Then, besides the food stamps, there are several religious organizations, both Protestant and Catholic, that give away bags of food to the poor. I hit those places too.

Food stamps from the homeless is also a good way to make money. I know where to stand in the barrio and meet the guys right after they get their stamps. I buy them for one-third the face value of the stamps and sell them for one-half or sometimes more in the barrio. They are happy to get the money for wine and I'm happy with my profit. Then I have my regular blood days two or three times a month at the blood centers.

When I was living in the barrio, I used to buy three or four cases of beer and several pints of wine every Saturday and sell them before the legal selling time on Sunday morning. I had an ice chest under some trees in an empty lot near downtown. I sold each can of beer for a dollar and the wine for two dollars. Don't worry about me. I get along pretty well on my own. ✜

3 CONTRABAND

*When I was a kid, I was blinded
in my left eye. Now that I'm older,
to avoid running into things, I
make wide turns, what we call
"Guadalajara" turns. In that city
you never round a corner directly.
You make wide turns because you
never know who's waiting around
that corner.*

—Rudy

DURING THE 1970S POLITICIANS
in Arizona and throughout the United States flirted with the idea
that some drugs, especially marijuana, should be decriminalized.
Perhaps in reaction to the tragedy that Vietnam became and the
excesses of the Nixon years, the majority of Americans seemed
caught up in a spirit of liberalism and a willingness to look at new
solutions to old problems.

In February 1977, Senator F. Felix, a Democrat from Tucson, introduced a bill in the Arizona Senate to reduce marijuana-possession
penalties. In March of the same year, the Tucson City Council
recommended that pot possession be reduced to a misdemeanor, and
on April 3, the Arizona legislature passed Senator Felix's pot bill.

In Phoenix, two Colombians accused of operating a heroin-smug-
gling ring were freed because the deadline for a "speedy trial" had
passed. In May, a poll in Arizona showed many of the residents
favored the legal use of small amounts of marijuana. This followed
the national trend. While Arizona Senator Dennis DeConcini was
urging the Mexican government to intensify enforcement of their
drug laws, the Arizona Criminal Code Commission was urging softer
statutes on this side of the border, and the Pima County Public

Defender went so far as to recommend that heroin be legalized. Despite this new mood of tolerance on drug issues, Arizona was gathering something of a reputation as a troubled drug center.

Reports were coming back from as far east as Connecticut, all the way to California and on to Washington and Oregon about Arizona residents being arrested for transporting marijuana, heroin, and cocaine. Tucson was already becoming known as a trans-shipment city in the early 1970s, especially for large marijuana shipments to the East Coast.

It was the aftermath of the Age of Aquarius, Woodstock, and the magic of San Francisco's Summer of Love. For the drug dealers it was still a time when transactions involving hundreds of thousands of dollars could be made with a handshake, when a man's word meant something, and honor and respect were of primary importance. The wholesale killings had not yet started.

♦ ♦ ♦

We sit in a narrow booth near the back at the Crossroads, a Mexican restaurant on the South Side of Tucson. It's almost noon, but there are plenty of tables waiting to be filled. This is a restaurant from the 1940s that was once known for its Tucson-style food, hot and spicy, nothing fancy, good prices, and the coldest pitcher beer in town. It was a drive-in owned by gringos. Now it's been remodeled, the food is styled in Sonoran fashion with fancy fish dishes and mild chilis. Memories flood my mind while Rudy checks out the room.

This was one of the places I often visited with Ed, Tommy, and Mike, rookie cops all of us, still scared this was all a dream. We came to unwind and savor the events of the night after working eight or more hours in a hot police car, chasing Yaqui shadows in Pascua Village, breaking up family fights on the South Side, investigating a shooting or a stabbing as the temperature soared and tempers got raw. Checking out the burglar alarm kicked off again by the wind, kicking some ass at the El Victoria Ballroom or the El Casino. Then writing the endless case reports. We drink our pitchers of beer quickly to beat the one o'clock deadline. Then we sit around the parking lot with a six-pack just talking cop talk, still pumped up with the excitement of that first good bust. A squad car goes by, starts to pull in, and then just blinks his lights. We toast him, comrades in arms, and there is a warm feeling of belonging to an exclusive club.

Rudy reads from the plastic menu that also serves as a place mat. A faceless waiter, looking very Mexican with black pants, a white long-sleeve shirt, scuffed shoes with ultrathin soles, and a bored expression, takes our order. The salsa is not great, too watery, too much garlic. For the first time I notice the murmur of people around us. The noontime crowd is coming in. Rudy unconsciously, or consciously, has taken the seat placing his back to the wall, the seat I normally would have tried to take, and for a moment I feel exposed. We both scan the customers as they enter, and it feels all right, so I relax. For me it's just an old habit that's hard to break. For Rudy it's survival. I look at him across the booth and I see a grandfather with white hair and a trim moustache, a steady working man who cuts hair for a living, and I have to remind myself where this man has been, what he had to do to successfully move drugs from Mexico to the United States, from the West Coast to the East Coast. And he made it big time. That he lost it all doesn't matter to me. I have to know how he came full circle back to the straight life.

✚ I was born and raised right here in this barrio. I had three older brothers and an older sister. Dad died when I was very young, so we were alone most of the time while my mother was working to feed us. We were very poor, just like everyone else in the damn barrio. I don't know anyone who lived here you could say was better off than the rest of us. Maybe that's why we were so united against the outside world. For instance, during the war the *pachucos* came in and tried to take over the barrios. They wore strange-looking clothes and ducktail haircuts, the pants, called "drapes," with pegged cuffs, and double-soled shoes. And they carried chains to scare everybody with. When they came to the Barrio Libre, we kicked the shit out of them, and then to piss them off we created our own style of dress. We wore white silk shirts with pearl buttons. The buttons had to be made of pearl, or they didn't count. The pants and shoes were just the opposite of the *pachucos'*, tight at the thighs, flaring out to bell-bottoms. Our shoes were patent leather, with pointy tips and paper-thin soles. We didn't need chains. The only *pachuco* thing that kind of stuck around was that special language they created, a slang that eliminated a lot of bullshit when you spoke it. Macho words that emphasized the meaning, like the word *ese* for hello, which said, "I acknowledge you," and my favorite, *chocale*, which was the word for shaking hands but intimated "grasp my hand like a man."

Everything was a struggle. All of the family had to work to help out, so I shined shoes, sold newspapers, cleaned yards, whatever it took. When I was thirteen or fourteen, there were always five or six of us from the barrio who would ride our bikes to the fancy houses in El Encanto neighborhood, out on the east side of town then. Now it's in the center of the city. We would clean yards and do gardening for the rich people. We went in groups when we left the barrio because it wasn't a very good idea to get caught going through another barrio by yourself. We would pick oranges or grapefruit from the trees in the front yards of the homes as we made our way back to the barrio.

My first and only heroes were my uncle Diego (my mother's brother who raised me after my father died) and a cowboy friend of his, named Pedro Moreno. From my uncle I learned respect and honor. He taught me to be good, to work hard for my money, to respect others so they will respect you. Pedro Moreno, on the other hand, could be a mean bastard when he was provoked. He always packed a gun and was sometimes on the wrong side of the law. Maybe because I was small of frame, like he was, he took a liking to me. From him I learned how to be bad, and he taught me that sometimes if you can't get a man to respect you no matter what you do, then make him fear you.

Pedro was tough. When he was about eighty years old, he used to go around on a three-wheeled bike. You might have seen him going up and down the avenue. He used to help out at the corrals on West Twenty-ninth, and one day they gave him a big chunk of meat that he took home and was going to hang on a hook on the back porch. He was a short man, so he put a bench in front of the hook to reach it, and when he went to hook the meat, the bench slipped and he fell forward into the hook. It pierced him under the chin and finally stopped under his jaw by his right ear. He hung there until help came. But he was a tough old bastard and he was all right except for a big ugly scar.

Pedro operated from a ranch owned by Lico Burrell near Three Points, south of Tucson. The ranch was near the mountain that looks like someone chopped off the top, in what they call the Valle de Altar. Pedro lived there and worked for Lico on the ranch as a cowboy, but, of course, his main source of income was from smuggling. They ran mescal and tequila from Sasabe through San Miguel to Tucson. This was in the early days of Prohibition, 1921 or around then.

The mescal smugglers of those early days created the routes that marijuana smugglers have been using for years and are still using to this day. The only reason they didn't bring in marijuana is that there wasn't any available in Mexico. About the only ones growing and using marijuana at that time were the Yaqui Indians of the Rio Yaqui, and they weren't sharing it with anyone. The first narcotic drug brought into the United States by the Tucson smugglers was opium. The first shipments probably started coming in during the early 1900s and continued until the late 1950s, when heroin was introduced and became popular.

Opium came in gum form that looked like soft tar. The addict would cut a little piece, put it in a pipe, and smoke it. Later on they started shooting it in their arms, dissolving the opium by boiling a little bit in water, using a spoon with the handle bent back.

When I was a kid I used to spend all the time I could with Pedro and my uncle at the ranch or at Pedro's house in town about a block from my uncle's house. They had horses there too, and while the other kids were learning to play baseball and learning to dance the jitterbug, I was learning to ride horses and be a cowboy.

School and I never got along very well. I didn't have anything against it, but it took up too much of my time. I left home the first chance I got, hitching a ride to California to work in the fields.

I was almost twenty-one when I finally graduated from high school. My brothers went after me in California and brought me back at gunpoint. They told me that I had to finish high school or they would just kill me. I believed them and in a year I was able to graduate.

I loved to hear the stories that Pedro and his friend told about bootlegging and the shoot-outs they had with the federal officers. The stories were about real men, one on one, shooting it out on horseback, real chases, running at full speed down mountainsides, through arroyos and across open plains, the smugglers unwilling to give up their booty, the agents determined to stop the flow of illegal booze into the country. I didn't need movies or artificial heroes. I had the real thing.

My uncle advised me to find a trade of some kind, and the easiest that I could think of was to be a barber. You can always find work as a barber, even when things are tough. So I learned the trade. I was doing pretty well as a barber and I was thinking about building a couple of houses to rent. I went out on a limb to buy all the plumbing for them. The only trouble was I didn't have enough money in the bank to cover the check I gave for the material. I knew the check was going to bounce on Monday and it was very embarrassing to me. I had never done anything like that before and always had good credit. Then this deal presented itself to me and I saw a way out of my predicament. It involved delivering some marijuana to a certain place and collecting some money. It was so easy and the money was unbelievably good. That's how it started for me, to pay off the damn plumbing on some houses I never did build. At first it was just a part-time thing, just when I needed some extra money to pay bills or for emergencies. ✧

In the late sixties things in Tucson had become very tight. Work was scarce and Rudy was tired of cutting hair. There was already a definite, calculated invasion into the United States by Mexican drug dealers to take over the distribution of marijuana and heroin. As more and more Mexicans crossed the border into the United States, the dealers got lost in the crowd; they entered the work force and moved into the old barrios where they were more comfortable, certainly more accepted, and totally inconspicuous. Before long they were sending their children to school, paying taxes and Social Security, and demanding food stamps, health benefits, and government housing.

In the meantime we started to see more drugs coming into Tucson and staying here than we had in years. After the Mexican mafiosos were established in the barrios, had found legitimate jobs, and had even started buying houses here, they started to make their move.

✤ At first they told the home-boy dealers that they were just making it easy for them to get supplies so they wouldn't have to take the trip to Sonora and take the risks involved in bringing the drugs back across the border. We were seeing more and more of the bastards in the street scene, in the bars along South Fourth and Sixth Avenues, especially at Danny's Hideway and the Ozark, the bars where most of the addicts hung out and made their deals. They started selling more and more directly to customers, cutting out the local dealers by giving more product for less money. There were some serious confrontations and people started to die. The home-boy dealers fought back by pulling some drug rip-offs. That is, getting the product on consignment and then not paying for it, or simply robbing the Mexicans of their drugs when they delivered them. We will never know how many of the poor bastards wound up in wells out in the desert. ✤

By the early 1970s the Mexican mafiosos had won the battle of the drug market by sheer force of numbers and economic pressure. The

Rafael Caro Quinteros and Jaime Figueroa Sotos could hire the poor *gauchitos* (poor peasants) to act as mules to bring the drugs across for almost nothing. If they got caught, so what? The supplier lost the product and that's all. There was an army of mules available who would kill for a chance to work. Once they were established, the mafiosos took off their silk gloves and pulled out their AK-47s. The home boys who weren't paying were dying. There was nothing they could do but buy from the Mexicans and behave themselves.

Faced with this ever-increasing invasion into his new way of life, Rudy came up with an innovative answer to his problem. He turned the process around by moving to Mexico to make his fortune.

✣ Through friends in the business world who are well connected in Mexico, I went to work for the Mexican government in Sonora. They told me, "This job is not available, but we have this or that we will give you." Before long I was working with the equivalent of our Department of Game and Fish to discourage the small ranch owners from putting out poisoned meat to kill coyotes. We tried to tell them they were also killing a great many valuable birds and other forms of wildlife and that it would come back to haunt them. It was a lost cause, even the local rangers turned the people against us, and a couple of times I was in danger of being lynched.

Those two years in Sonora helped me a great deal to meet and make friends with the people I wanted to become involved with and who I hoped would help me make money. I was fortunate to come under the protection of Don Leopoldo Fernandez from Chihuahua, who controlled the area where I was assigned. So, when the poisoned-meat project was canceled, there I was in Mexico; I had made influential friends, and I decided that my fortune was before me.

At first I never sold anything, not even marijuana. I was in the growing end of the business. Selling wasn't my job; I was in supply. I was sent up into the mountains with some others to contract with the Indian farmers to grow marijuana for us.

This was in Sinaloa as you are going south toward Culiacán. About half an hour before you get to Culiacán, you go west and then up into the Sierra Madres. Where we went up to the fields, there was a river that was deep and about a block and a half wide at the bottom. The current was strong. By the time we reached the top, we could jump over it without getting our feet wet. This trail leads to a ranch owned by my sponsor, Don Leopoldo Fernández.

As we climbed, the road just disappeared and we traveled the rest of the way either on burros or on foot. The security was everywhere. It was impossible not to feel the eyes that followed every step we took. Near the ranch we started meeting the armed guards. We would see them standing by the side of a hill or perched in a tree or just sitting on a horse. All were armed with automatic weapons, *bandoleras* swinging across their chests and the ever-present .45-caliber automatic pistol they love so much in Mexico. Hard, unsmiling *vaqueros*. Some were Indians, strange looking in their traditional baggy pants and white cloth shirts, long straight black hair held in place with a folded bandana across the forehead. The very modern-looking AK-47s were strapped to their shoulders next to a machete hanging from the waist.

I hate to think what it would have been like if we hadn't been friends, if we had been trying to enter without permission. Once we crossed the river at the top, we stepped into another world. In a clearing surrounded by trees was the ranch house, designed in the Spanish style. Many archways, sparkling fountains in the courtyard, beautifully tiled mosaics covering the floors of the verandas that led into even more elaborate tiles covering the floors of the spacious living rooms and bedrooms. Inside the house every modern convenience known to man was available in every room. The kitchen at the bottom of the U-shaped building would serve the finest restaurants of Europe.

Behind the house near the corrals, a paved landing strip made possible easy transportation for those allowed to land or leave. The parties and fiestas held at the ranch were legendary and often included dignitaries high in the Mexican government who rubbed elbows with the cream of the Mexican and Colombian mafias. Unfortunately, on this trip we were on business that would take us even higher into the Sierra Madres.

After leaving the ranch we really went up into the mountains where the land doesn't belong to anyone who can't hold it. Here there isn't any water to be found except from the seasonal rains, yet it is even greener and more verdant than below. It was tough, dangerous, and very difficult work to talk the farmers into not growing the things they had planted for centuries in these mountains. They couldn't understand why anyone would plant a product that couldn't be eaten or given to animals to eat. This was my chance to prove myself, to show them a Mexican from Tucson could do anything they could do. Before long everybody who planted anything around this small village was working for us.

We even brought in some American hippies to show them how to cultivate the plants, to grow sinsemilla, a new seedless strain of marijuana perfected in California. If we had left it to them, they would have grown ragweed.

At first the mountain people were not very friendly, and I remember that we never saw any of their women unless they were very old or just children. The Indians who were farming for us were very possessive of their women and we had been warned that they would kill us if we even dared to look at them in a suggestive or covetous way. The smartest thing I did was to start a store for them right there in the village. It wasn't anything fancy, maybe twelve feet wide and thirty feet long. We made regular trips to Tucson for batteries, canned goods, used clothing, and just about anything they needed but couldn't get. We gave it to them just as barter, a courtesy, so they would keep growing for us. After we did this for them, we became good friends, and they seemed to gain a great deal of respect for us. We only had a radio for entertainment, so in the evening, after supper, my partner and I went to the store and sat on the front porch on some old captains' chairs. Every night the people of the village came by to pay their respects. They would line up in front of us and we had to shake hands with everybody in the village. After a few weeks we started seeing the younger women in the greeting line.

Later on they started wanting guns and ammunition, and this caused some trouble. We would go to bed early, but the men of the village would stay up drinking and come to the store, which also served as the cantina, and they would yell and scream and shoot up in the air. Most of the time they were just having a hell of a good time. When they fought, it was with machetes, the more traditional weapon of the people in this area.

The most difficult thing we had to do was to build a runway for small planes on the side of the mountain. Because of the terrain, the runway tilted uphill. The planes had to land going uphill and take off going downhill. All of the work on the landing strip was done by hand, using the men of the village to cut the trees and level the ground. At the end of the growing season the American dealers brought in their small planes and we loaded them down as much as we could. It was tricky flying because there wasn't much room. Those damn pilots were good.

Don Leopoldo dealt mostly in heavy stuff, but he was also the connection to the *commandante* of our district. It's kind of hard to explain, but essentially this is what I mean: Every district in Mexico is protected by federal, state, and local police. The federal police, or *federales*, run the whole show and are under the command of a district *commandante* who is usually a military man with the rank of colonel or above. Nothing transpires in any of these districts without the approval of the district *commandante*, and this includes illegal transactions. In all of the time I was working in Mexico I never knew nor did I attempt to find out who the *commandante* in that district was. You see, I was working on my own, but I paid Don Leopoldo for the right to work under him and he in turn paid the *commandante* who was in charge of the territory. Once I made the right connections and paid my dues, I was allowed to work anywhere in that district.

For instance, I was sent to this village by Don Leopoldo's people, I stayed two seasons, and then I was moved someplace else. You can't do too much in one place because the word gets around, and if you become too well known, you might fall prey to some independent cop trying to make a name or a few extra bucks, or hoodlums and highwaymen who might do you harm.

This was probably around 1974, when I was younger and just learning the trade, long before I went to Guadalajara and made the contacts that allowed me to start dealing in Quaaludes [methaqualone pills, a powerful prescription sedative]. This eventually became my only line of work. I worked alone, even though from time to time I did have investors when I wanted to make a big purchase. It's impossible for me to tell you how I made my contacts and started selling Quaaludes, but when the opportunity presented itself, I grabbed it. The main ingredient used to make Quaaludes is manufactured in France, at a large pharmaceutical house that is strictly legitimate. Every so often a batch of the drug from France disappears and ends up in Guadalajara at a well-known legal pharmaceutical house where it is reprocessed for the illegal market.

I will tell you this much: My contact was the president of the company. When I needed the product, I called his office and made a luncheon appointment with his secretary. We often met at the best restaurants in Guadalajara, had a nice lunch and a few drinks, which I paid for, and as he was preparing to leave I passed him an envelope with the money. We would hug like old friends and he would whisper a location where my product would be. I usually purchased 175,000 pills at a time at a cost to me of eighty-three cents a pill. Then all it took was calls to Detroit, Chicago, and San Francisco. Setting this up took about three weeks to a month. When the deal was set, I packed the pills in five suitcases and booked a flight from Guadalajara to one of those three cities. I sold the Quaaludes for $1.75 each. This brought me a profit of $161,000 about every six weeks. You can see I was doing all right. Of course, that's not including my overhead and paying my helpers, but that wasn't very much.

My best customers in San Francisco were the Italians, who are big in the seafood business on the wharf. In Chicago it was the nephews of Al Capone, who do not work together but are very close. In Detroit it was old man Gregarous, who is part Greek and part Italian and controls the food industry in that city. He's the one who introduced me to the Italians. ✦

Rudy was on top of the world, with his fancy cars, luxury homes in Mexico and the United States, a thirty-eight-foot boat docked in one of the fanciest marinas in Guaymas, Mexico, designer clothes, snakeskin boots, more money than he could spend, and best of all, the women. They came in every shape, form, and color, all of them eager to please the dynamic little drug dealer on a short frame with a big bankroll. Not bad for a pint-sized boy from one of the poorest neighborhoods on the south side of Tucson.

✦ When I was dealing, when I was in what we call *la movida*, or in the business . . . well, this isn't a story I'm proud of. It's more of an anecdote, something that happened to me once, in a time of my life that's over. My Quaalude buys in Guadalajara were maybe $100,000 or $150,000 worth of merchandise at a time. It was the summer of 1978. For some reason the manufacturer had not been able to complete the entire order, so I stashed what was available in my apartment and waited for the rest of it so I could bring the entire shipment in one trip to my customers in the U.S. One of my people told me about three guys from Culiacán who wanted to buy from me. I needed to protect myself from losses at this point, so I agreed to meet with them and sell them as many Quaaludes as I had available. There were three of us: Juan and Lugo, who worked for me, and myself. Juan said the buyers were OK. Late that evening we went to the address they had given us to see if we could make a deal.

The apartment wasn't like the apartments we know in the U.S. There were apartments and stores next to each other in a row. They do this because land is very valuable in Guadalajara and they don't waste any space. In order to get to the front door, we had to go down about three steps, and I noticed as we walked down that there was another apartment to the right, but it was dark and looked empty. I reasoned that these guys had rented the apartment for the purpose of this sale only. As we walked down the steps, I started feeling uncomfortable about the deal. I was glad I hadn't brought the merchandise with me, a necessary precaution in these transactions. Two guys were waiting for us, and after we sat down they said the guy with the money was on his way. Another warning light flashed in my head. It was obvious after a few minutes that they were stalling, so I told them I was going to wait for them by the car where the merchandise was. I motioned to Juan and Lugo to stay with them so there wouldn't be any funny stuff and to make sure they didn't try to follow me.

I went outside into the protection of the night and sat on the curb near my car with my pistol by my side and waited to see who was going to show up. I loved the lush green lawns, tall trees, and the wide boulevards of Guadalajara in those days. If it had not been for the business at hand, I would have sat back and enjoyed the cool of the night.

About fifteen minutes later I heard one shot, and then another one. I retreated farther into the night and waited. I lost track of time, then I heard someone whistle from the apartment. One long, one short, a sound so ominous it made my skin crawl. Still I waited for some sign from my people. After five more minutes my friends still didn't show themselves. I crouched low and ran to my car and raced to my apartment for some help. I stashed the merchandise in a safe place, called for some *pistoleros* who had been recommended to me, and we rushed back to the apartment. About an hour had elapsed since I heard the shots.

Juan and Lugo were dead, the bogus buyers gone. They had both been shot in the back of the head, both in the same place behind the ear as they sat on the sofa. I remember noticing that Lugo had bled very little, while Juan bled all over the place. Lugo's eyes were open and he had a confused look. We removed their wallets and any form of identification the police might use to find out who they were. I didn't want Lugo's family to find out how he had died. His father was a general manager for a large company on the U.S.-Mexico border. They were a very rich and nice family who had always tried to help Lugo. For some reason Lugo had formed vicious habits. Juan I didn't care about. He was born vicious and had been bad all of his life.

The men I called on to go back to the apartment with me were Paco and a guy we called "Johnny Negro," even though Johnny wasn't black. Paco was not in the drug business; he was a member of the *Liga Veinte y Tres de Septiembre*, a terrorist group dedicated to the overthrow of the Mexican government that went around robbing banks and blowing up gasoline stations and government buildings. Johnny Negro was just a *pistolero* who helped me from time to time.

The two men who had tried to rob me were known to them. They were from Culiacán. After we stripped the bodies, we returned to my apartment, and Johnny Negro selected two men and they went after the killers who were racing for home.

Let me explain something. I had not lost anything, the robbery had failed, so I was out of it. When Johnny asked me what I was going to do about the killers, I told him I wasn't out anything, so I wasn't going to do anything. Since he was working for me at the time and Juan and Lugo were his friends, he asked for permission to go after them. I told him to do what he had to do. They caught them on the highway before they arrived in Culiacán and killed them on the spot. The matter was settled. Johnny Negro, I assume, called ahead to Culiacán and had some people waiting for them outside of the city. That's what I would have done if I were chasing them.

A few days after Lugo and Juan were killed, the rest of my order was filled and I brought the shipment to Tucson. I called the people in San Francisco, Detroit, and Chicago, loaded my suitcases, and flew to those cities to deliver the Quaaludes.

About a year later I gathered a group of people to bring some marijuana from a small pueblo in Nayarit. We were getting the pot through a friend and associate by the name of José Luis who lived there and practically ran the entire town. He was the *patrón*, the boss, and we bought from different people through him. José Luis, Johnny Negro, and I were in this together. Johnny Negro had two people with him from Denver, Colorado. One of them was a Puerto Rican, a *pistolero*. I had my *pistolero*, Pancho Pistolas.

We left Tucson in two vehicles, both of which belonged to me. Johnny Negro and one of his bodyguards left in my van, and José Luis, Pancho Pistolas, and I left in my new Camaro. The plan was that we would drive to Culiacan and from there to Guadalajara. I would stay in Guadalajara to buy some more Quaaludes and Johnny Negro and one of the gunmen from Colorado would go on to Nayarit with the van to buy the marijuana. José Luis, Pancho, and the Puerto Rican were going to go on to Mexico City to see about making another transaction. It was all proceeding according to plan. We had hidden $85,000 and some guns in the van for Johnny Negro to pay for the marijuana. He and his friend from Colorado left in the early afternoon. The others left a few minutes later for Mexico City, and I settled in to have a nice time in Guadalajara until my Quaaludes were ready.

That night Johnny Negro and his friend checked into a motel before they reached the Nayarit state line. Sometime during the night they were pulled from their beds in the motel room by several gunmen and they were shot forty times. Inside the motel-room bathroom police found two or three hundred dollars scattered about the blood-stained floor. Outside they found the van, but my $85,000 and the guns were gone.

Now things start to get messy and confused, and I have to make you understand that a *pistolero* has only one master, that's all, and if he isn't that way, you don't want him. The only thing he has to think about is his master and that's the way you want him to be. The Puerto Rican was an especially bloodthirsty killer, and he was not only Johnny Negro's bodyguard but his friend too. When he found out that Johnny had been murdered, he went into a rage. He had been living on uncut cocaine for three months, and he told José Luis and the others that he was leaving and there was no way they could stop him. For some reason that only he could understand, he believed that I had something to do with killing my own people for my own money.

José Luis called me in Guadalajara and told me what had happened and that the Puerto Rican was coming my way. He didn't know, or failed to mention, that the crazy bastard blamed me for Johnny Negro's death. The Puerto Rican went to the scene of the murders, took the van, and drove to Tucson. I left Guadalajara the same day, but I had a load of Quaaludes and had to drive more carefully, so he arrived in Tucson before I did. As soon as Pancho Pistolas, my *pistolero*, heard what had happened and about the Puerto Rican, he left for Nogales to await my call.

Several days later I was in the backyard of my house on the far west side of Tucson, working in the garden. This was my castle, I felt safe there, and I wasn't really thinking too much about what had happened in Mexico. I was pushing a wheelbarrow full of vegetables from the garden to the house. My wife was with me, walking a little behind with my four-year-old son, when my van—think about it, *my* van—came in through the gate and stopped next to me. The next thing I know the door opened and there was a man standing next to me with a sawed-off, doubled-barreled shotgun in my face. It was the Puerto Rican.

"You're going to go with me," he told me.

My oldest son was in the house where all my guns were, and I thought, if he sees I'm in trouble, he's going to get a gun and try to help me. And this crazy bastard is going to kill him and all of us too. So I told the Puerto Rican not to cause any trouble, that I would go with him. I whispered to my wife that I was going with him and if

I didn't come back or if they found me dead to tell the cops who I left with. She knew about these things, and even though she was scared, she just nodded her head and grabbed our son to her side. The Puerto Rican opened the door of the van for me and I got in. Then he told me he was going to kill me. His eyes were cold as ice and there wasn't any doubt in my mind that he meant it. He wasn't thinking clearly, he had been doing a lot of coke, and I guess he blamed himself when his master was killed. He had to have revenge on someone. The only reason I went with him was to get away from the house and my family.

Once we left the yard, he pulled over to the side of the road and threw a pair of handcuffs at me and told me to put them on.

"Put them on behind your back," he told me.

I tried to talk him into letting me put them on with my hands in front, but I could see he was getting mad again, so I lifted my right leg and told him I would put the cuffs underneath one leg. That way I couldn't run or attack him. This was what he wanted anyway and there wasn't time to argue. He tightened the one on my left wrist, but when he went to tighten the other one, I pulled the links tight with my leg, so when he clamped them shut, he caught most of my upper hand at the widest point. This left the cuffs loose and I could slip out of them easily by squeezing my fingers together.

We drove off again, with the double barrels stuck in my ribs, both hammers pulled back. I couldn't help but think that if he hit a bump I was dead. I didn't have much time left and I knew it. We drove all the way into town. He told me he was taking me to his girlfriend's house. I felt a glimmer of hope when he told me who she was. I knew her, she's the granddaughter of an old friend of mine, a prominent businessman and a very successful politician. I knew him to be a good man from a pioneer family, highly respected in both the Anglo and Mexican communities, a state legislator for many years. When we arrived at her place, I told her, "Tell this bastard to turn me loose, and we'll forget the whole thing happened." Uh, uh, she said, and I said, oh, oh. She had been my last hope. Up until then I thought I was going to get free of this shit, that she would help me because of who she was.

But at least she didn't want me killed at her place and made him take me away from there. We headed out in the van again. When I looked up, we were coming to a busy intersection on the north side of town, and he was in the inside lane as we approached a red light. As soon as he slowed for the light, I started working the right cuff loose, and as soon as he stopped, I swung it at him and hit his ugly face. At the same time I kicked the door open and jumped. The last I saw of him, he was holding his head in his right hand and making a turn at the light to come after me. I was running behind the St. George's Buffet restaurant with the handcuffs dangling and banging at my legs when I spotted a young guy with his girl sitting in a car outside an apartment. "Someone's trying to kill me," I told them. "Can you get me out of here?" The guy was real cool and took me all the way home even though I had just asked him to drop me off on the South Side.

I knew if I could get to my home turf I could get plenty of help. I paid the kid for taking me home, and the rage started setting in. The handcuffs were still hanging from my wrist. I couldn't walk around with them dangling and banging on my legs, so I went to AAA Lock and Key to get them off. It was late at night and I went to the locksmith's house in back of the shop and banged on the door until he came out. I told him some stupid story about playing with the kids and losing the key. He didn't begin to believe me, but he was used to weird things. It took him ten seconds to find a key and get the cuffs off. He charged me ten bucks.

On the way home I made the sign of the cross and thanked God for sparing my life one more time. Then I did something foolish. I lost my temper. In the business I was in, this was not a good thing. I brought out some guns and went looking for the Puerto Rican bastard who had the balls to try to kill me in my own van. But he was long gone, I couldn't find him. I called Pancho Pistolas in Nogales and told him to come home. He left immediately with his brother

Tony. The way it worked with my *pistoleros* was that every time I bought a house, I always bought a place close by for them. I paid the rent, the utilities, the food, and paid them five hundred a week besides.

We found out where the Puerto Rican was staying, but every time he came out, he was with his girl and her two sisters, always hidden among them. We didn't want to hurt them and start a bloodbath, he was the only one we wanted. Pancho Pistolas was staying with his brother at a house I had rented for them in Tubac, a community about forty minutes south of Tucson. I had rented the place there to use as a stash-house. If I needed him, he could make it to my house in less than an hour, and I didn't think the Puerto Rican was foolish enough to come after me at the ranch again. But he wasn't finished with me yet.

A few days later I was sitting at home when the phone rang. My son answered and came to tell me that Trini wanted to talk to me. I knew Trini, a kid, casually through his mother who I'd known for years. I had no reason to talk to him, so I told my son to tell him I was out. Trini called several more times and finally I talked to him. He wanted to invite me to a party. He said there'd be a girl there who wanted to meet me. I told him no. He was desperate, and it came across over the phone. Party, hell—it was the Puerto Rican giving the party and I was the guest of honor. Finally I just slammed the phone down and pulled the plug.

Sometimes it's best to follow your instincts. Later I found out that the Puerto Rican had tortured Trini to force him to lure me to his house. He had tied Trini's hands behind his back and was holding the phone to his ear every time he called me. Every time Trini failed, he banged him in the kidneys. When the Puerto Rican realized that it wasn't going to work, the bastard killed Trini. Blew his head off with that shotgun. They had to bury the poor kid without a head. When they found Trini's body in a girl's apartment on Miracle Mile, I'll be damned if the police didn't come out and pick me up for investigation. They had questioned a friend of Trini's and for some reason he involved me.

Hanging out in Tucson, 1970

Downtown, 1980

Transient, 1971

Looking for action, 1984

South Tucson, 1972

Convent Street, 1972

Sunday morning, 1972

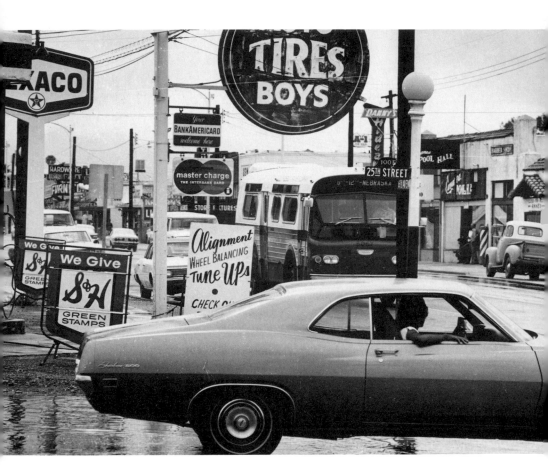

The South Side, 1971

Rainy season, 1972

Drying out, 1971

South Sixth Avenue, 1972

Walking the street, 1989

Strawberry, 1972

Still around, 1979

Photography by David Burckhalter © 1990

So there I was, under investigation. They took my statement and turned me loose. Later they caught the Puerto Rican in Colorado and brought him back for trial. A jury found him guilty. The judge sentenced him to twenty-one years and allowed him to serve his sentence in New York under the pretense that there he could be close to relatives. The real reason was that we had people waiting for him in the Arizona prison system. The granddaughter of my friend, the pioneer politician, received three years for her part in Trini's murder. It seems she drove the getaway car. When the Puerto Rican gets out, who knows what will happen. ♣

Rudy's wife was gorgeous, just gorgeous. Long legs and the prettiest face you'd ever seen. Rudy truly believed he'd found the perfect woman. After she had his kid, he had married her, and they were happy. Five years and a couple of kids later he took her to live in the large two-story Spanish-style hacienda Rudy owned on the west side of town.

But as soon as he went out the front door, she was bringing someone in the back door. They say the husband is the last to know, and if Rudy wasn't last, he was near the end of the line. What really pissed him off was that she was pointing her lovers right at his business.

♣ Chickie, Lalo, and the other "friends" would come to me and ask me what I was doing. They knew I had something going because I was making big money, and it bugged the shit out of them that I wouldn't let them in on my action. Lalo was the heavyweight, if there is such a thing among these dumb bastards. So to get to me, he went after her whenever I was out of town on business. She was sleeping with all of them, the same people who were trying to cut in on me, and she told them where I was and everything I was doing. Part of that was my fault for trusting her, but I guess it's natural for a guy to come home from work and share his experiences with his wife.

Anyway, she not only told them everything, but she gave away several pounds of my personal marijuana, a suitcase full of Quaaludes I was going to deliver on my next trip, and worst of all, she gave her lovers all of my "flake," a really high grade of Peruvian cocaine that cost me a fortune. The divorce was short and bitter. ✛

The murder of "El Indio," a twenty-eight-year-old suspected drug dealer, didn't get more than a blip on page seven of section B in the *Arizona Daily Star*. He walked out of his house, the killer drove up and parked behind him. He walked back to the car to talk to the driver. Neighbors heard a shot ring out. El Indio staggered back to the kitchen door as the killer's car backed slowly out of the driveway. "I've been shot," he told his wife and fell halfway into the house. For nine days El Indio fought for his life, and then he died. He died without identifying his killer. A year and a half later Rudy was arrested in Nogales, Sonora, and charged with first-degree murder in the shotgun death of El Indio.

✛ I used to cut El Indio's hair when he was a kid. My mother lived just a few blocks from him on the same street. I didn't have any reason to kill him. If I had killed him or anyone else because of jealousy over my wife, I would have had to kill half of the South Side. I had never done any business with him and he didn't owe anyone money that I know of. There was no motive to tie me to the murder.

What happened was that at this time in my business I had to do things to some people in Tucson for nonpayment of debts. Sometimes they owed me for this and that, and sometimes friends in Mexico would call and tell me, hey, this guy owes so much, will you take care of it for me. I picked up these guys that owed money and I made them pay. In these matters I always worked alone. I wasn't the kind to take three or four guys with me to collect. Since no one was with me when I did this collection business, no one knew what I did to them. These people I collected from had started a hate group against me. But I didn't care because nobody bothered me, you know.

I knew they were lying about me, and they knew they were lying about me. They were able to convince certain people that I was the guilty one. Among them was an uncle of El Indio, an important drug dealer in Sonora. He was very fond of his nephew and did not take kindly to the killing of his relative.

But these bastards didn't know the real me until they pissed me off. If you say something about me or commit a bad act against me, I'm going to go to your door and settle it there, or you're going to go with me and settle it anywhere you want. I never take anyone along to help me.

Consequently, all these people were mad at me and wanted to get even with me, so when this shit went down about the murder, all of them said, Rudy did it, Rudy did it. Pretty soon I had three or four guys hired by this relative in Mexico looking for me with guns. I had to get the fuck out of here. The first thing I did was to send my daughter and my ex-wife to the police to see what the hell they had against me. At that time they didn't have anything on me, but they led my ex-wife and daughter to believe they did. Finally, the grand jury brought an indictment against me. They had twenty-six witnesses who all said they saw me do it or heard that I did it. One witness said that this woman had her ear against the door and heard everything that happened. It wasn't true, nobody knows what happened, nobody has been told the truth about what happened. The first thing El Indio said when his wife asked him who shot him was, "I don't know."

Alibi, why do you need an alibi when you're innocent? I still had to get out of town, or get killed, so I went to Mexico to hide out with my good friends and business associates, known in Nogales, Sonora, as the "Chimichangas." These same people, my friends who were selling me pot, sold me out for five thousand dollars. El Indio's uncle is a powerful drug dealer, much bigger than the ones I was dealing with, so they sold me out. There was a murder warrant for me in Mexico. The *federales* surrounded the house and took me into custody. They were all disappointed that I wasn't armed.

I was in jail for over ninety days before I could make bail. The bond started at a quarter of a million before my lawyer had it reduced to one hundred thousand and I made a property bond. My ex-wife came to see me and asked what she could do. I asked my lawyer and he said, "Marry her." I did, and now she didn't have to testify against me. The county attorney tried to have it annulled, claiming she and her relatives had received death threats if she didn't marry me again. The judge threw it out, and that's as close as we got to going to trial in this case. At first the county attorney offered to plea-bargain for twenty-five years, then ten, then six months in the county jail or time served. We said no, let's go to court. Then the case was dropped. The county attorney said that his main witnesses were coerced and wouldn't testify. ✤

Shortly after the charges were dropped, Rudy came home and found his wife taking a shower with another woman. The next divorce was even quicker.

For Rudy the business was no longer worth the risks. The character of the drug dealers was changing. There was a new breed, and a lack of respect and honor among the dealers themselves. So Rudy folded his tent. In the short time that he was on top of his game, Rudy managed to own the fancy cars, the four-wheel-drive pickup trucks, the boats, and the wrought-iron-wrapped homes expected of a major-league drug dealer. He rubbed elbows with the cream of both the drug empires and straight societies here, in Mexico, and in Central America. And he gladly gave it all up.

The murder trial, the affair in Mexico, the divorces had left Rudy in bad shape. The money was gone, but he had lost the desire to start over.

✚ For me the money had lost its value, it didn't mean anything anymore. I could buy anything I wanted and not worry about payments, taxes, or where my next meal was coming from, but it was nothing to me, it left me cold. So now I cut hair, go home, and sleep better than I have for years. The temptation is always there. Sometimes when things are going bad, when I have a hangover and don't feel like going to work, or the kids call and they need money, I know that the big money is only a phone call away and I cringe at how bad I want the good life again. Then I think about the kids, about my grandchildren, and I go to work and forget about the cars, the clothes, and the women for another nine hours.

There is this Jewish woman from Detroit who was a big customer of mine. She lives in Tucson now, her father is one of the leading investment brokers on the East Coast. Recently he bought her a half-million-dollar house in the Foothills. Somehow she found out where I was working and came to see me. She's in her thirties now, and for old time's sake I scored some pills for her. We dated and the good life was awfully tempting again. I hope I can stay where I belong.

I don't think about it anymore, don't miss it—the cars, the boats, the women, nothing. It seems like it was something that happened to me in a past life and is forgotten. I never think about it, and if people come to me and say, hey, help me with this or help me with that, I just laugh at them because I know what they're in for. I don't make as much money, but I don't need it. I sleep good and I don't worry about anything except for a few people who have tried to pick me up.

Retiring from the business is not always as easy as it seems. The profits are still enormous, which makes the taking of risks tempting, but there are also drawbacks. It's a business where making enemies comes with the territory.

The murder case against me was thrown out of court, and as far as the State of Arizona was concerned, I was innocent and could not be tried again or punished for the murder. But there was another who had judged me guilty—El Indio's uncle was not willing to accept the verdict of the court. He lives in Sonora, but his arms extend across the border whenever he pleases.

There have been three attempts to kill me. The first when I went out for a newspaper. A van came driving by me and a guy got out. He made the mistake of leaving the door open and the engine running. I noticed that. The guy walked into the Circle K behind me and bought a paper too. Instead of letting him walk behind me, I went behind him and pushed him out the door while I hit him with the paper. He got scared and jumped back in the van while I walked away. I knew he wouldn't kill me in front of a lot of people. He had to get me in the van first.

Another time I was waiting for someone to let go of the pay phone out there on the street and I saw three guys coming in a car. Immediately I knew what they were after. They were after Rudy. I didn't have a gun on me, but it was only two blocks away, so I got back in my car and put it in reverse to get under the light so I could see who they were. I knew who they were, and they knew I knew. They kept going and I saw them go into a restaurant. So I went home and got my gun and went back to the restaurant. Now things are different, I'm armed and they aren't. They let themselves get into that position. Dummies! I let them know it.

The third attempt almost got me. I had gone to a bar on Park Avenue near Irvington. I checked the bar, looked all the way around as I usually do, and I didn't see any strangers, so I went ahead and ordered a beer. She was just another bar hooker, a little spent but still attractive enough to work the bar for drinks and whatever the traffic will bear. When she sat down next to me, I didn't really think too much about it. I bought her a drink for old time's sake and we made small talk about unimportant shit between two people not trying to hustle each other. I relaxed and settled in, turning my defensive attitude down a notch until she bought me a beer and said she was going to go to another bar down the road for a minute to pick up a girl who was dying to meet me. When she left, I walked to the restrooms and opened both doors. They were empty. But then I failed to follow my instincts. I should have walked out the door as fast as I could and got the hell out of the area. Instead I went back and sat down.

When she came back, she was alone, the girlfriend was going to join us in a few minutes, she said. She even pulled another stool next to us and I ordered another beer. In a few minutes, before the beer even arrived, she stood up and walked away. I felt a hand on my arm. It was this guy Chickie who sells cars for a big car dealer here. "Hi Rudy, how you doing," he said and put a ten on the bar to buy a drink. I turned around and there is a guy behind me, a big fat guy I knew from years ago. "Hey Rudy, can I talk to you outside a minute?" he asks me. Sure, why not, I answer him, and I know right away I'm fucked. He was walking in front of me, so as we're going out I took my knife out of my pocket, opened it up, and slipped it into my jacket pocket. As we went out the door, someone grabbed me from behind but up high around the shoulders, too high. I could still reach into my jacket pocket. The guy in front turned around and put a gun to my head and said, "Let's go."

I said, "No, you son of a bitch. If you're going to kill me, you're going to kill me here and now. You're not going to take me out there and knock the shit out of me and then kill me." This was all happening fast, but to me it was slow motion. I reached the knife in my pocket, pulled it out, and stabbed the guy who was holding me from behind in the stomach. So he went back, taking me with him. I stabbed him again and he went back another step. Now I had him against the wall. He was holding me, but he was against the wall. The guy with the gun was aiming it at me, but he didn't shoot me, and right away I knew he didn't know what he was doing. When something like this happens, you immediately hit the victim in the neck area to paralyze his arms, or you hurt him somehow, but this guy didn't know. The man holding me had to let go because he was hurting, but he tried to grab me again and I hit him again in the stomach and it went in deep.

About that time two girls came out of the bar and when they saw what was going on, they ran back inside screaming. The guy with the gun ran when he saw the special cops they had working as bouncers come out. The guy I stabbed looked down at his shirt that was covered with his blood and yelled, "Look what the old man did to me!" The bouncers came toward me and they weren't smiling. I was the victim, and they think I'm the bad guy. Oh shit, all I wanted to do was get away from them. The guy I stabbed didn't have any legs under him with all the blood he'd lost, and the bouncers didn't chase me very far. I got in my car, took out the gun I keep under the seat, and drove around the block. Now I'm madder than hell. I wanted to get those bastards. I spotted the fat guy hanging around behind the bar, so I stopped my car and started to walk toward him, but first I whistled at him and he whistled back. The whistle means I challenge him. He whistles back, he accepts. As I walked toward him, the light of a passing car or the moon gave off a glint from the barrel of my gun and he hollered, *"Anda cuetillado,"* he's armed, and he started running. He was going down Park Avenue running like hell. I heard a truck, and before I could get back to my car, it picked him up, and then all I heard was the sound of screeching tires burning the asphalt. Then it was quiet.

I have never seen the fat guy again. I've been to his mother's house, to his sister's house, and every place I can think of, but he's gone. The one who was holding me, who I stabbed, was the son of a guy who grew up with me in the barrio. We started in first grade together, and though we haven't been close, we go back a long way. When the kid was better, I called my friend and told him to keep his son away from me or I would have to bury him. My friend still comes to the barber shop and he doesn't say anything to me. Why should he? His son was wrong. I thought by calling him I was doing the right thing, because if I didn't and something happened, then I would have him on my neck.

The guy who said hello to me first, the one who sells cars, he's the one who fingered me to those guys. I know he's the one that paid them. If he fingered me, he paid. My intelligence and my instincts tell me he fingered me, but I can't prove it. I wouldn't even try. What for? Why did he do it? I don't know why. I think I know . . . the relatives and friends of El Indio never forget. ✤

The August wind is hot and muggy from recent rains that tease but don't do very much good. The swamp cooler in the barbershop is not helping. Only those desperate for a haircut will sit under the barber's apron. My conversation with Rudy proves that a bumper sticker I once saw is right: "Smuggling isn't just a job, it's a way of life." Rudy talks about an article in the morning paper a few days before, about American customs agents at the Douglas, Arizona, crossing who had caused four thousand dollars' damage to an RV when the drug-sniffing dogs indicated interest in parts of the vehicle. The man and his family had a bitch in heat, and this was what the dogs reacted to. Rudy is not smiling. The same thing happened to him last month, but he doesn't have a dog.

Rudy had arranged for two thousand pounds of shrimp from Guaymas, Mexico, to be brought across illegally. Rudy and his car are well known to the customs computer, so when he showed up at the border, they pulled him over and tore his car apart. One agent tore the ceiling liner almost off—now it just hangs there limply. Rudy was clean, he only had fifty pounds of shrimp with him, the legal limit allowed. The agent who did the most damage disappeared, and about an hour later another agent handed Rudy a claims form and told him that he had to bring the car to a shop across the street on Monday if he wanted it fixed. The agent turned his back and walked away without an apology.

Rudy smiles. The two thousand pounds of shrimp had already been transported to Tucson earlier in four other vehicles. The fish were already in the buyer's freezer. The weekend in Guaymas had netted Rudy a four-thousand-dollar profit.

✤ In the business of contraband the most important thing is experience and contacts. You have to know who to buy from—and have a buyer ready to receive the merchandise. Naturally, you have to have the cash to make the deal and the people who are going to do the transporting. This takes organization and planning. When you're ready to make your move, everything has to be in place and ready to move at a moment's notice. Now that everything is in place, you need two more things for a successful operation, luck and secrecy. You don't tell the seller where you're going or the buyer where you came from. If no one knows, they can't catch you. ✤

4　EVERYWHERE I TURN

I have a good job, I'm respected in the community, my friends are accountants, lawyers, and doctors. It would be tragic for me to take a bust. But if I can make a few extra bucks, why not?

—Kevin

IN THE GOOD OLD DAYS IT WAS rather simple. Everything seemed black and white like our television sets. Drug dealers stayed in the barrios and the ghettos. They were to be pitied, but there was nothing really important to worry about in our bright new world. In the fifties and sixties, the straight world had enough problems with alcohol and new evidence that cigarette smoking was probably bad for your health. The thought of having to give up smoking was traumatic enough to make a lot of us look for a safer way to relax.

Tranquilizers were the answer. Family doctors were the original drug dealers for harried businessmen, overworked housewives, as well as the rich and famous. As early as the 1930s, jazz musicians and nightclub comics were known to smoke marijuana. The comic and the musician were portrayed in movie after movie as the tragic but lovable characters who usually wound up dying in a tear-jerking final scene. It set the mood for things to come in America.

Now everywhere I turn I bump into drugs. At every level, from the street punk to the stockbroker, the need is the same. The drugs once confined to the slums and the barrios have overflowed into mainstream America, from the Corn Belt to the Sun Belt and every place in between. In a back alley or a penthouse, the kick is the same.

◆ ◆ ◆

Gary

It was the middle of September and we were sitting in Gary's small office. He owns a limousine company and he was lamenting that business was off because he hadn't had any runs for his drug-dealing clientele for quite a while. He guessed that the drug war was really having an effect and the town was drying up. I assured him that the marijuana harvest season would soon be upon us. Then the boys would be buzzing around town making up for lost time, and they would once again have pockets bulging with money.

I remember Gary when he was a kid running around the ambulances his father owned, pretending he was driving them on high-speed runs. Gary grew up big and strong. He looks like a linebacker who visits the training camp lunch table too often. Gary wears thick glasses and is a sharp businessman when he has to be. Although he seldom drinks more than a beer from time to time and never does drugs, he seems to get a kick out of talking about the drug dealers and the adventures they have in his limos. He loves to tease and has a sharp memory for detail, remembering down to the alligator boots the way his customers were dressed and what kind of gold jewelry they were wearing.

✦ A call comes into my office at ten o'clock at night. A guy with a Spanish accent wants a limo until four or five in the morning. By talking to my customers a few minutes, I can usually tell what business they are in. People who are involved with drugs never give a last name, it's always "Huero," "Chapo," or sometimes we get a "John Smith." Drug people don't like to leave a paper or plastic trail, they always pay cash. They carry lots of money with them. If they run out of money, they go back to the house and get some more. The places where they live are typically in good shape, usually in neighbor-hoods that aren't so nice. When you take them out, they spend big money on things people don't normally spend money on, and they tip big. When they first call, they want the limo for two or three hours and invariably will keep it six or eight hours.

You never know what they are going to do. They are so unpredict-able. You might start a run in Tucson and wind up in Nogales, Sonora, or Phoenix, and we have had them hire the limo to take them to Las Vegas or Los Angeles just to watch a fight. Money is never a problem. If they damage something on the limo, you give them a price and they pay for it in cash. Your typical drug dealer spends money like it came very easily to him. They usually go to the topless bars, and when the topless bars close, they usually pick up some dancers and take them to somebody's residence, or they go cruising. It's been my experience that they don't do drugs in the limo. When they go out, it's to spend money and drink. They sometimes have cocaine or marijuana with them, but it's usually to give away to friends or to impress people with, especially the topless dancers. They use cocaine to lure the girls into going out with them.

I ask these people what they do for a living. Some say they are in investments or some say they do landscaping or wrought iron. And their favorite answer is they own a body shop or a bar. Another thing that tips me off to what they do for a living is when they want to go to a liquor store for some beer, they give you twenty dollars. The bill comes to six dollars, and you keep the change. They might do this four or five times a night. We get them in all ages too. Young guys in their twenties, middle-aged men, as well as young junior-high and high-school kids. You know where the money came from. You know if you pick up a fourteen-year-old kid with three or four hundred dollars in his pocket to pay for a limo, either he's in the business or his dad is.

But it's not something you can count on for the survival of your business. Sometimes they will call you every night for two or three weeks straight, and then they drop out of sight for six months. Then they come back again for another fling. Sometimes another crop will come in and a new group of people will emerge. You have them for a little while. They use you pretty regularly, and then they go away. By and large, though, it seems to be pretty fashionable among Mexican drug dealers to hire limos for just about any social function they might have. Weddings and *quinceneras* [a religious ceremony and social occasion in the Mexican tradition that is celebrated when a young lady turns fifteen] are big, but we have been hired for baptisms or some kid's first communion. We take them from the church to the rented hall for a reception.

We get all kinds of personalities. They're always talking about doing something legitimate with their money. I had this one guy who was renting limos all the time and was getting to be a pretty good customer. One night he tells me, "You know what, I'm going to buy a ranch. I'm going to have cattle on it, horses, pigs, and chickens. I'm going to put some money in that." That was on Thursday. He told me to have a limo at his house at 5 P.M. on Saturday, said he was going to be busy all week buying these animals. I had the limo there at five o'clock and he said he'd been to Marana in a pickup truck with his buddies and they had bought two calves, some chickens, and a few pigs. He didn't have the land or a ranch yet, but he had the livestock. We went to this dumpy house on the West Side, and the lady who lived in the house, his aunt, asked him what he was going to do with the animals he'd dumped there. "I'm going to leave them here until I buy my land," he told her proudly. That was about the last time I saw him, and I never did find out if he bought the ranch.

Take Huero, for instance. Huero likes to go to a bar, start a fight or yell at people, nasty things, and then he runs like hell for the limo and we have to take off with people running after us.

I met Huero through a friend in the drug world. He seemed to be a pretty nice guy, but I knew he had a very short temper. When I talked to him or was with him, though, he never caused any trouble. I mention him because he is a prototype of the drug dealer we see so often. They call him Huero [blond] because of his light skin and light brown hair. He is close to six feet tall, early twenties, speaks excellent Spanish and pretty good English. He has no visible means of support, but drives a nice car, lives in a nice house on the east side of town in a minibarrio away from the South Side where most of the dealers prefer to live. This drives the cops wild. They would rather be able to keep tabs on them without driving all over town. Huero doesn't have much of a future, but he'll ride the roller coaster until the cops or the competition knock him off.

Huero picked up this dancer one night, took her to the Tack Room for dinner and then to a bar for a drink. When they walked in, she said hi to a guy she used to date. Huero blew up, wanted to fight, the whole nine yards. Finally we got him out and into the limo. Huero and the dancer fought back and forth for a few blocks, then I heard a bang from the back. There's a center-mounted champagne bucket that fits into a minibar over the axle hump. It's made of polished wood and cost me plenty. Huero had come down on the minibar with his fist and shattered it. He kept yelling at the dancer that he had a gun and was going to shut her up for good. She was holding her own, but I finally had had enough and took them back to the bar where her car was. I told him the minibar was four hundred bucks. Without blinking an eye he whipped out a roll of bills and gave me four one-hundred-dollar bills and another hundred for a tip. When I left them, they were walking arm in arm into the bar.

They always claim to be armed. You'd certainly hope a guy like Huero is lying about packing a gun because he's so unpredictable and quick-tempered. You don't know what he's capable of doing. Another thing I've noticed about guys who deal drugs is that they seem to know a lot of people and they enjoy the notoriety—and adulation they get from straight people. For the most part they seem to prefer the topless bars because the girls flock to them and make them feel important. Even if it's all just for the tips.

I had these guys one night who I knew were in the business. We had made numerous stops all over town. One guy would get out of the limo, go inside a house, and come out in a couple of minutes and we'd go to the next stop. Anyway, I finally took them to this topless dancer's house, and she put on a private show for them. They paid her a couple of hundred bucks and we left. I know there wasn't any sex involved afterward, and again this seems to be typical. It doesn't seem to be a requirement. It's as if they just want the attention from them and to be seen with these good-looking, well-built girls.

A call came in the other night to meet a party at a supermarket parking lot. The guy gives me a name, assures me he and his friend will be there. This is a common practice. We almost never go to their houses. We get calls to pick them up at hotels, nightclubs, or just out at some intersection. Most of the time we don't take them back to where they started out. This is especially true of customers who make frequent stops in all parts of the city. Sometimes they rent two limos. One follows the other, and a lot of times there isn't anyone using the trailing limo. They rent two in case they meet people they want to take along with them. You can see that money has no value to these people.

Listen, not all the drug dealers are Mexican. Two of my best customers were a couple of white students in their early twenties attending the University of Arizona. They live in an expensive apartment in the Foothills, they drive Porsches, and it's all one big party. They usually call late at night, spur-of-the-moment calls, and they might want to go to Santa Monica or Las Vegas. One night the head guy called and wanted a limo right away. He'd just wrecked his Porsche and needed transportation, so he rented a limo for six or eight hours. Paid cash. They seem to have an endless supply of money on them. They like to party like the Mexican dealers, but they aren't flashy and don't wear all the gold jewelry. There are some who don't want it known that that's what they do, and then there are the ones who want everyone to know. The ones who do the most talking and make the most noise are the ones who don't last very long. But these guys with the Porsches look like typical college kids out on the town with daddy's money. You would never suspect them.

You know, you can't tell anymore who's selling drugs or using drugs. The people you least suspect are doing it. They said on television recently that there was a thirty-percent reduction in the use of marijuana and thirty-five in cocaine and that fewer people are using drugs, but I don't know if that's true or not. It doesn't seem like it. Fewer users but more addicts, and heroin seems to be making a comeback. ✤

Beau

We met for the first time at the University of Arizona library. I was digging up some more of my roots and reliving the past at the Special Collections section when I first laid eyes on Beau. He looked so damn scholarly and wise, yet he grinned with his eyes as he worked on his research paper. He seemed interested in what I was doing and we talked about it. He was a good listener and it helped my ego that someone wanted to know about my people. Over pizza and beer I found out he was a university graduate, married, no kids, and lived close by. His accent intrigued me—so much Southern, mixed with Western. After that we just became friends, and he never failed to help me with my stories, good or bad.

Beau should have been born Mexican. He loves to party, loves pretty women, good music, a good story, playing poker, drinking beer, and, most of all, putting off until tomorrow what absolutely doesn't have to be done today. He had been an officer in Vietnam and had seen and knew more about what happened with drugs among our troops, whether they were majors or privates, than most people ever will.

✤ I arrived in Saigon near the end of 1970. I was an Army lieutenant in military intelligence. My salary made me a millionaire by Vietnamese standards. My rank and title gave me the documents to travel anywhere in South Vietnam without too much hassle from the military police. The Army even gave me a jeep to tool around in.

More important to my situation was the program Nixon called Vietnamization. That meant that most Americans, save some hard-core advisors, special-forces-type units, career spooks, Marines, and who-knows-what kind of mercenaries, were being pulled out of combat and placed in support roles. The plan was for more native boys to get killed instead of American boys.

The rear-echelon bureaucracy was getting pretty bloated by the time I got there. It was four months before they even found a job for me. I went over in an airliner full of second lieutenants, and most of us seemed to end up whiling away our time until the system could concoct something for us to do.

There I was: twenty-three years old, money in my pocket, time on my hands, and the most depraved city on earth before me. If my parents had known, Richard Nixon would have got a couple fewer votes.

It took about twenty-four hours to figure out that everyone was abusing either drugs or alcohol. There was a division of intoxicants that generally held true: the lifers, that is career officers and non-commissioned officers, boozed to excess; the enlisted men and junior officers took drugs. The line stood between generations as much as between ranks.

Saigon was a rich scene—everyone was drunk, stoned, armed, and pissed off about where they were. Lots of hostility. Lifers, heads, blacks, whites, Americans, Vietnamese, Chinese, Australians, South Koreans, spooks of every stripe, young Saigon cowboys lusting after our wristwatches, cameras, and wallets. And doubtless lots of Viet Cong. All hating one another in a town where every day is the worst day of summer and the garbage strike is permanent.

The biggest army we faced was made up of young prostitutes. A sixteen-year-old girl could make more in a night than her father could make in a month.

Now, to give you some idea, I had a maid six days a week to wash and iron my fatigues, polish my boots, keep my room in the bachelor officers quarters (for the most part Saigon hotels commandeered by the U.S. military) spotless and crisp, clean sheets on my bed—all for about twenty-five bucks a month.

It was a fine place to be if you were young, single, and male. The only drawback was the incessant terrorism and the inclination of a lot of people to use all those guns they had. You could play it safe, go to your room every night, stay off the streets, keep to heavily guarded U.S. mess halls and clubs. Or you could check out the city, the countryside, the whole exotic scene, and maybe get sniped or blown up.

Drugs put up a pretty fair barrier between your common sense and the danger. Most of the guys I knew took their chances and hit the streets, the fine restaurants, the nightclubs on Tu Do street, the whorehouses, the massage parlors ("Steam 'n Cream" joints they were called), the fabulous open markets, the zoo, whatever. Essentially we were a dazed mob wandering around in a Disneyland of vice.

Every drug—except for cocaine—was as close as the nearest street stand or cab driver. The marijuana was stronger, more intoxicating than anything we had ever been exposed to. Pot of that quality wouldn't be available to Americans until the mid-1970s, when Northern California sinsemilla growers got their industry off the ground.

A pound of top-quality Thai buds went for around fifty bucks. Everyone's favorite, however, was the opium-laced pot sold in cigarette packs at virtually every street stand in Saigon. For ten bucks you got what looked like a straight pack of cigarettes. Winstons, Kools, whatever, the cellophane tightly wrapped and sealed as though the pack just came out of a carton. Inside were twenty perfectly rolled, cigarette-sized joints. The opium gave them a special quality and taste, and they gave a dreamy kind of high that went well with the tropical heat.

I remember the first time I smoked that pot. A couple of enlisted men approached me, said they'd heard I was cool. We split a joint out in a graveyard on the outskirts of Saigon, near where our unit was stationed. I'd smoked pot in the States, and at first this stuff didn't seem that special. Then I went to their hootch and it hit me. I tried to read a three-panel Dick Tracy comic strip in the *Stars and Stripes* newspaper. All I could see were abstract black and white shapes. It made no sense at all.

The pot, strong as it was, was fairly benign compared to what else was available. The same cab driver who scored some smoke for you was just as eager to get you some opium or heroin—both of the finest quality. I smoked both on occasion, and it seemed that as long as you inhaled it, and didn't do even that very often, you could get home without a habit. Unfortunately, too many guys looked for that ultimate high—and I've got to say that shouldn't surprise anyone. We were bored most of the time, we were very young (some of my men were in their teens), we hated what we were doing. Most people in the rear (REMFs we were called—Rear Echelon Motherfuckers) had senseless jobs, most opposed the war. We were alienated, hot and sweaty, we knew we were missing the hippie scene and the sexual revolution back home, and we felt a huge amount of guilt about the few Americans who were still in the field battling an excellent army of men who wanted to kill them. You put young men in those circumstances, and you should expect many of them to seek an escape.

Heroin is the best escape in the world. And Saigon's was the best heroin in the world. Pure shit from the Iron Triangle. I admit that even smoking it gave a complete body high and took away every worry you'd ever had, but I hated the stuff. It was a solitary high, it made you absolutely nonsocial. We would roll out the first half-inch or so of tobacco from a Kool cigarette (it had to be a Kool for some reason), fill the gap with white heroin and light up. In the meantime, the guys who shot it were cooking, fixing, sharing a needle. Pretty soon what you had was a bunch of guys lying around on filthy mattresses and pillows in a steam-hot room not talking to each other.

Each in a private, silent high. In fact, they got really pissed off if anyone came around them.

One day, one of my troops came up to me with what looked like a Hershey bar wrapped in foil. It was the biggest chunk of opium I'd ever imagined. He said it cost twenty-five dollars from a cab driver. We smoked that shit for a week, and everyone reported wild dreams each morning. It was a powerful downer, but more of a social high. You could function, move about, and talk to people.

I guess the wildest thing around was the LSD, usually brought back by guys from California who had been on leave back home. It was amazing how casually guys dropped acid. I was to meet some friends one night at some seedy apartment one of them shared with a young Vietnamese hooker. It was going to be a party, and one of the troops gave me a tab of acid when I went off duty. Unfortunately, as it turned out, I dropped it on my way over to the apartment. I got there first, went in, relaxed, and waited for the stuff to come on. Well, that night a storm blew into Saigon that had even the locals running for cover. It rained so hard the windows of the apartment were blown out and the rooms began to fill with water, probably three inches deep on the floor. Of course, electricity was knocked out all over the city. It didn't even take a storm to do that. The power was off in Saigon a lot. The streets were filled with emergency vehicles, cops of every kind all over the place. My friends didn't make it.

I was stuck in this water-filled rathole of a place—I mean that literally, rats were climbing up the furniture as the water rose— alone, in the dark, with a head full of acid. Pretty soon I found myself talking to some really nasty version of my own personality, a royal, carping asshole sitting across the room from me. And this asshole knew every hidden guilt within me. You can't win an argument with an asshole like that. It was the worst night of my life, the only time I ever truly considered suicide—just to get away from whatever the acid let out of me. That was the last acid I ever touched.

I guess it's obvious that I did drugs with my troops. They were my friends. I wasn't a traditional officer in that regard. All any of us wanted to do was get home. Our jobs were pointless. I don't believe even the Army gave a shit about that war by 1971. I did take care of my men, did my best to help them out, keep them out of trouble so they could get home honorably. I had a half-dozen men who had unbelievable heroin habits, and I got all but one of them clean for the urinalysis everyone had to take before getting on the big bird back to the world. One guy, a fellow from Chicago, was hopeless though.

This guy tried for about a half-day to quit, then decided, fuck it, he was going to score higher on the pee test than anyone who had gone before him. He went on a weeklong fix, and he flunked and ended up in the hospital. After a couple of weeks in rehab, they came to pick him up to take him to the plane. I swear he managed to score some skag between the hospital and the runway.

In fact, of those five who got home clean, all but one resumed their habits back in the U.S. I contacted them when I got back, they admitted it, laughed. If anyone tells you Vietnam didn't create a lot of drug users who brought their habits back to the world, they're full of shit. ✛

Rene

Rene's mother was a prostitute, his father was a drug dealer, both were junkies. When I was a cop, I spent a lot of time trying to bust them. Rene is tall and thin, he seems to always need a shave and smells of cigarette smoke, but other than that he's not bad looking. He has about nine children, but only five live at home, and some of those aren't his. Nothing seems to bother Rene. He has a loose and easy quality about him mixed in with layers of potential violence straining for release.

In the early 1970s, a few of the Cuban refugees brought to the United States by President Carter made their way to Tucson. The Cubans tried to take over the drug and prostitution scenes, and attempted to start a protection racket on the South Side. That they are a wild and violent people there is no doubt, but when they came to Tucson, the home boys were ready for them.

Antonio, the dominant Cuban, tried to extort money from Lydia, who owned a Mexican restaurant on the South Side. She appealed to Rene for help. He went to work right away, making an Uzi-type automatic weapon. Then he shot the shit out of Antonio's car. When that didn't get the message across, Rene took a shot at Antonio with a sawed-off shotgun. Antonio managed to push one of his bodyguards in front of the buckshot coming his way and didn't get hit. The bodyguard lost an eye and Antonio got the message.

That's the way Rene is. He doesn't have any money, he doesn't do drugs or drink. Rene takes food stamps, food baskets, and anything he can get for his family, and still he can't make it. It's almost impossible to keep track of his address because they move so often.

In a tight situation there are few people I would trust to watch my back more than I would Rene. In the barrio you learn to take care of each other like family. Just because your brother owes you money or lets you down in a small way, you don't put him down. If I lend Rene money or do him a favor, I know he's going to pay me back in a hundred ways.

✤ They call Pete Lopez "Gato." I had known him through my parents as a kid, and out of respect for him and my dad who worked for Gato, I called him uncle. Talking about big-time drug dealers in the Southwest, Gato was high in the top ten during the 1970s. There were others, of course, who were probably bigger, but to me he was the top man. Late in 1973 Gato asked me to help them transport some drugs on a big deal that was going to come down south of Tucson. I refused, but I told him that I'd ride shotgun for him. Gato looked at me and laughed. Here I was, over six feet tall and skinny as a toothpick. I was always very quiet and mild-mannered, and I was asking to be one of his guns on a deal this big. I asked him again. Gato saw the look on my face and finally told me it was OK, I could go.

The deal went down, but it went down badly. We had driven south towards Nogales in three cars, with three guys in each car. One was the lead, the second the money car, and the third the back-up. I brought along a few hand grenades. [To this day, Rene is known on the streets for the bag of grenades he owns.] At the Amado turnoff we went west toward Arivaca, a very old ranching community in the middle of nowhere and right in the middle of some of the oldest smuggling routes in Arizona. Mostly for booze and drugs coming to Tucson from Mexico, and for the gun-running Yaquis of old going the other way. A few miles out of the town, which only has a bar, a store, a school, a post office, and a few houses, we met with the dealers from Sonora.

They came with their *pistoleros* for protection and they came in separate cars as we did. We had the money, they had the heroin. On the way to our meeting place I was in the last car, Gato in the center, and the rest of our people up ahead casing the road to make sure we hadn't run into a trap.

When our people signaled it was OK, we went ahead to the agreed place. We stopped about twenty or thirty feet from the first car. Gato got down and their main guy did too, and they met about halfway. They walked off to a brushy area where another car was waiting. Gato signaled us to follow and got in. We drove for some time until we passed a small lake. About three miles past the lake we climbed to a ridge and stopped. Gato and their man were walking toward us and I heard them arguing. It didn't feel right, I sensed that something had gone wrong. I started backing away and told the others to get ready, something was going to go down. I was looking for some cover when Gato turned around and floored the guy with one punch. He dived for his car and Gato's driver started backing up as fast as he could. The shit hit the fan; it seemed everyone started firing at the same time.

I grabbed my small bag of hand grenades. I threw one, then

another. I heard a man scream and knew he'd been hit by fragments. From the back seat I pulled one of our automatic weapons and emptied it on their cars. Gato screamed for us to get the hell out. Two of our guys took off running into the brush, and I dived into the car and we hauled ass. Their guys were also getting the hell out of there in a hurry, taking their wounded with them. We met later at a place called Half-Way Station that was once a way station for the stagecoach lines between Tucson and Nogales. The other car had picked up our people and when we met with Gato, he told us that he'd got all their *chiva*, our name for heroin, and still had his money. The heroin was the black tarlike heroin, not the powdered kind.

My dad wasn't with us on this run, but I wanted to prove to him I was a man and could handle myself in these situations. I wanted him to be proud of me. The plan was for us to separate once we had the *chiva*, and my dad would be waiting for it in town to distribute it to the pound- and ounce-dealers working for Gato while we went to Gato's house at the new Yaqui village on the south side of town called New Pasqua. Gato was more than generous with me when it came time for my share, probably because of my dad. He handed me twenty-five thousand dollars just for being his muscle. ✣

Kevin

Thirtyish and well built, Kevin is a classy dresser and the ultimate pleasure seeker without the great income he needs to be considered a true yuppie. He sometimes rubs elbows with bankers, college presidents, and high-rolling new car dealers. Kevin is invited to a lot of parties through contacts he and his wife have at the University of Arizona. But he needs a few illegal dollars to be able to stay in these social and political circles. So he occasionally provides cocaine and marijuana to close friends who want to spice up their lives and party with drugs. Kevin is able to move with equal ease among his Mexican connections and his high-brow friends even though he comes from the Midwest and is a relative newcomer to this area. This surprised me at first, but I had a chance to talk to Kevin at an old-fashioned baptismal party on the South Side where he and his wife were the only Anglos, and they seemed to blend right in. Kevin knows how to get along with people no matter what their station in life.

♣ What I was doing is technically illegal, I guess, but, hey, I made some money, I bought some things. I was able to landscape the whole lot, I bought new furniture, a little at a time. We didn't buy a car outright, but I made enough for the down payment and we were able to take care of the monthly payments without a strain on the old budget. The main thing is, I wasn't blowing it up my nose. I made money and it was safe as hell. The ones who become heavy users are the ones who go down. One of our friends lost his job, his house, and it almost got him divorced. But instead of quitting, he went into selling drugs full-time. He's dealing maybe nine, ten ounces of coke a day and sometimes a little pot. He feels he was wasting his time working for a living. I don't know, maybe because he's not a big-time dealer, the cops haven't bothered him yet. Or, it might be because he's working within a network where he sells only to people he knows—friends, relatives, people he trusts. Very little chance of getting busted from within his own network if he stays inside of it, if he doesn't get greedy for that extra sale to someone he doesn't really know. But then there's always the chance of someone having an accident or getting caught with a paper of coke in his wallet. Nine times out of ten the cops will give the guy a choice of going to jail or giving up his source. Who gets caught and can't afford the scandal—you know what he's going to do.

My deal was different. I don't think I was doing anything that would be easy to prove, so I doubt the cops would have gone after me very hard. Hell, people go to swap meets and sell junk they know is bogus, broken, or even stolen, and then scram. Anything to make a buck. Believe me, these are hard times. But this isn't happening just in Tucson—it's all across the country as well as south of the border in Mexico.

Especially in Mexico, where the people are very poor. They have nothing to lose, so they become mules bringing dope across the border. Let me tell you something, these people will kill you in a second if they feel threatened or if you owe them money, or if someone pays them a couple of hundred dollars to get rid of you. They just don't care, life is cheap. They're working for their family, it's a matter of survival. And we have a lot of poor people here who will do the same thing. I mean they'll take a chance. If they get caught, so what, it can't get much worse.

I have to be careful. I have a good job, I'm respected in the community, my friends are accountants, lawyers, and doctors. It would be tragic for me to take a bust. But if I can make a few extra bucks, why not? I like that easy money.

When I first met Filiberto, he was working at a funeral home hauling flowers to the cemetery and doing odd jobs, cleaning the cars and going after death certificates. It wasn't much of a job, but it was just a front anyway. He wasn't interested in a career as a mortician. About three years ago he called my office and asked if I would be interested in making a little money. We met for lunch. Talking about making money is my favorite subject.

He wanted me to rent a car for him for a few days and then take it back when he was through with it. The way he described it, I couldn't turn it down. It sounded like such a sweet deal. All I had to do was rent a car using my credit card. Then I was to have a set of duplicate keys made for the ignition and trunk. After the keys were made, I would drive to a designated place, usually a shopping mall. I would lock the car and meet my friend in his car close by. I would give him the duplicate keys, he would give me two hundred bucks plus the cost of the rental, the keys, and any other incidental expenses I might incur. Then he would give me a ride home or I would take a cab.

He was honest with me. He told me straight out that he was

transporting marijuana from Tucson to a funeral home in northern Arizona and from there to the East Coast. Once the marijuana was loaded into the trunk, the rented car was driven to northern Arizona and parked in the garage of a funeral home where he had a friend. The next day Filiberto was taken to the train station. He took the marijuana, which was loaded in suitcases, and boarded the Amtrak train for Buffalo, New York. In Buffalo he was met by his contact. He was an Oriental gentleman, the owner of a restaurant. He met Filiberto at the Amtrak station and drove him to the alley behind the restaurant. They usually entered through the kitchen and took the suitcases to his office where the exchange was made. The money for the marijuana was paid, counted, and placed in a money belt that Filiberto strapped around his waist. It was usually thirty or forty thousand dollars. That same day Filiberto flew back to northern Arizona, someone from the funeral home picked him up, and he drove the car back to Tucson.

I kept the original keys while the rental car was driven to northern Arizona, always followed by another car. If for some reason it was stopped and the marijuana discovered, the back-up car would call a contact with a CB radio and tell him what was coming down. They would contact me by phone, and I would immediately report the car stolen. Luckily, it never happened.

My cover for renting cars so often was that I was an insurance salesman and supposedly traveled to all parts of Arizona on business. It was beautiful; I even deducted the rental expenses and gas from my income tax. If Filiberto was ever questioned, he would use the story that he was a skier going up for the winter sports. In the summer he was escaping the heat for the weekend.

It took at most three and a half days to get to Buffalo and return to northern Arizona, and then another day and a half to return the car to the rental agency. I always wanted to take it back myself because most of the time I found nickel-and-dime bags of pot and seeds all over the floorboards. I always took the car to a car wash and vacuumed it out, especially the trunk. Besides, the first thing they did when they got the car was to remove the little stickers Hertz and Avis put in the front and back window. Nothing was ever said about that, but I could always say it must have happened at the car wash. No use taking any chances. Also, I was paid fifty bucks more for taking the car back.

They preferred I take the car back because the people who were running the operation on this end were young Orientals and therefore more noticeable, and Filiberto was a twenty-two-year-old who looked seventeen. They were the people making all the deals and had the connections in Buffalo. I had occasion to meet the main guys, the Orientals, and they were students at the University of Arizona. Every time I had any dealings with them, they were with a white guy who dressed like a biker. You know, a rough-looking character with big shoulders, the long hair, tattoos on his thick arms, the colors on his vest. However, once he spoke, you knew he wasn't what he appeared to be. He was very well educated, just like his buddies. Nice people, friendly, no problems. What a slick operation they had.

The marijuana was coming out of Mexico, no doubt about that, but the way they had the network set up, the marijuana was coming into California or the Yuma area, and then it was going north to Portland, Oregon. From Portland it went to Salt Lake City, and from there it was trucked down here in rented vans, just like we did with the cars. Why they went this way I don't know. The theory was that if the load was going to get popped, it would probably happen before it arrived in Tucson. They took the northern route to Tucson through Flagstaff, and then backed up that way to the funeral home. They went to a lot of trouble, but it sure worked. They were never busted in the two years I worked with them and, as far as I know, haven't been busted to this day. I stopped renting cars for them last year, but we are still friends, we still see them at parties and social gatherings from time to time.

The way the marijuana was packaged was kind of neat. First it was wrapped in tons of cellophane, then heavily sprinkled with carpet cleaning fluid, and then placed in a trash compactor. When it came out of the compactor, it was half the size. That way they claimed they could get about forty pounds in each suitcase. Filiberto always had these old suitcases with lots of stickers from all the ski resorts and places he'd traveled. He often took his wife with him and offered to set up a deal for me to make a few trips. He made about six hundred and fifty for each trip, plus expenses, of course. He said they needed my face. I guess they felt I looked older, more businesslike, more distinguished with specks of gray in my hair, and I'm well groomed, I know how to dress.

But I didn't want to get greedy, didn't want to take any chances. I guess I should have, but I never did. Then Filiberto did get a little greedy, he started using too much cocaine and wanted to be cut in on the action. He was tired of being a mule. He wanted to be a distributor and have someone else take the chances. His wife got pregnant and couldn't travel anymore, and then he lost his job because he was doing too much coke, and finally he moved to Florida. Then I heard he joined the Air Force and was sent to Germany.

These are very careful people. I know the operation was still going on less than a year ago, but they have never bothered me or tried to force me back to work as has happened to others I know. Yet if I ever wanted to start again, I'm sure I could, just by picking up the phone and having lunch with one of them. Sometimes I'm tempted, but so far I've managed to stay away. About a year ago I ran into one of the Orientals at a Chinese restaurant on the east side of town. He wasn't eating, just hanging out more or less, which made me suspect he owned the place or had money in it. He came to our table and bought us a drink, wanted to buy us dinner, but I told him I'd catch him next time. He understood.

Buffalo seems to be the distribution point for a great deal of the marijuana that comes from Mexico. Why they picked Buffalo, I have no idea. Maybe because it's not as hot as New York City, or because it's out of the way. The group I was involved with was always going to Buffalo, but they would always fly back out of New York. I often asked myself why marijuana, when cocaine is so much easier to handle? In retrospect I could see the logic to handling the bulkier marijuana. In the first place, cocaine is hot right now. Most of the big busts you see are all cocaine or crack. Marijuana is just a step away from becoming legalized, at least in the minds of most of the middle-class users in America. You read about a cocaine bust on the front page. A marijuana bust is lucky to find itself near the obituary column or the crossword puzzle. ✤

5   GOOD COPS, BAD COPS

I saw it go from peace, love, and
flowers to guns, greed, and death.
                    —Pete Pershing

IT USED TO BE CALLED THE
Bureau of Narcotics and Dangerous Drugs when I was a cop. It
changed to the Drug Enforcement Agency in 1972, and the complexion of the agency changed from street-cop tough to paper-cop
efficient all over the country, with exceptions like Enrique Camarena, the agent who was murdered in Guadalajara by Rafael Caro
Quintero and his people. The way it used to be, you could call the
Bureau of Narcotics on the phone and talk to anyone in the agency
on a first-name basis. Call the DEA today and ask who you're
talking to, and they play spook games, as if revealing their names
would betray a classified secret and expose them to instant danger.
Maybe it would, given the attitudes among *narco-traficantes* who
ignore the taboos of previous underworld empires, which dictated
that you never kill a cop because of the heat it creates.

◆ ◆ ◆

It's been a long time since I wore a badge, and it isn't my intention
to make a case against anyone, to solve any crime, or to put anyone
in jail. The people who appear in this story talked to me because

they trusted me, and they trusted me because I always tried to be fair. In my thirteen years as a cop I never put anyone in jail who in my mind didn't belong there. I never knowingly lied on the stand or did anything contrary to accepted police procedures just to make a bust. It was a different time, with a different type of criminal. It was more personal, more one-on-one, and everybody more or less played by the rules. There was a sense of honor among thieves, tarnished as it might have been, but they didn't go around killing each other and the cops like they do now. The people and the courts trusted cops more in my day; the criminal element didn't always respect the man, but they respected the uniform and the badge.

For me it started in 1951 and lasted until 1964. I loved every minute of it. Some people look all of their lives and never find that special niche for themselves. I found it early and rode the merry-go-round as long as I could. It's a job that's sometimes a more demanding mistress than any woman could ever be, a job that some people never get out of their system. You try not to be a cop, but old habits are hard to get rid of.

The most dangerous, most thankless job in police work, next to responding to a family disturbance, is working as an undercover cop. He's the guy living on the edge, pretending to be something he isn't, the consummate actor dressing differently for every role he plays, speaking the lines as if his life depended on it, and it often does.

There are three sides to every story: the police version, the criminal's version, and what really happened. Things have a way of developing during the course of an investigation that requires an undercover cop to decide how far he can legally go to make his case. Sometimes you have to bend the law to make the jigsaw pieces in the case fit. You aren't who you're pretending to be, and nobody, especially the person you want to bust, can know that. So you lie, you wrap yourself in lies like they were your clothes. Maybe you have to dangle some bait to make your man take the lie in his mouth and swallow it. You know you've touched on a gray area called entrapment, but this particular drug dealer is guilty as hell and you want him bad. Maybe you did plant the seed in his mind in order to make him sell to you, but eventually he was going to sell to someone anyway. When you make your case report, you just leave that part out of the story.

When you're working under deep cover, you're out there practically by yourself. You have to cover your own ass the best way you can, and you always have to remember: you're only as good as the last case you made. If you don't get the job done, you're going to be back on patrol or sitting behind a desk making out missing-person reports. To the real undercover cop, that's just not acceptable.

To what lengths should the undercover cop go to maintain his cover? In Dallas recently, an undercover police officer watched a group of men rape a suspected prostitute but didn't try to stop them because he didn't want to blow his cover. He told the men who committed the rape he was sick to avoid having to actually participate. To what lengths should a cop go? I don't know, there aren't any written rules to go by. The officer in Dallas was wrong, we all know that. There has to come a time when a sense of decency kicks in, no matter how deep into your cover you have gone. That she was a whore didn't matter.

One of the First

Long before we heard of Frank Serpico, the undercover cop who achieved fame exposing corruption in the New York City police department, there was Joe Berume. Joe was one of the first to work deep cover in the barrios during the first big drug explosion right after World War II. Too many of our war heroes were coming home hooked on morphine. They found their addictions on the battlefield, in government hospitals overseas, and in VA hospitals right here at home. Joe was a hero in his own right and later was the oldest Marine from Tucson to volunteer for the Korean War. He was working with us at the Sheriff's Department. On one occasion I failed to recognize him in the drunk-tank at the city jail, but so had the city narc who arrested him, and he had known Joe all of his life. He looked bad, smelled bad, and had a mile of tracks on his skinny arms. He did a lot of time here and there to keep from blowing his cover. Then came the inevitable rumors that Joe had slipped over the edge, was doing drugs, doing burglaries, and selling dope like the scum he was trying to bust. Before he knew it he was back in uniform.

The Game

The narcs go under cover and try to infiltrate the ranks of the drug dealers, and the dealers try to guess who they are. Niggie finds out that the narcs are parking their cars at the back of the new police station downtown. He also knows when they change shifts. Niggie walks by and takes down the license-plate number and description of every car parked behind the PD. He walks back to the barrio and sells the information for a dollar a car from a phone booth next to a Chinese grocery.

Good Cops Don't Fix

Olivia is a little too fat right now. She was just released from the county jail where she served three months and ate too much good food. Olivia is thirty-seven and a confirmed junkie and prostitute. She used to be so damn pretty, but when I ran into her last month, all I could see was that she was short, fat, and dark. I looked at her again and noticed the needle tracks and swollen veins on her arms.

She's been married a couple of times, has an old man at Wilmot Prison doing more time than he can finish in this life, and three kids from three different men. One of the kids, the little girl of seven, was born with a heavy-duty methadone habit. Olivia was dropping 120 milligrams of methadone a day at the time. The baby was having convulsions and cried constantly. The nurse told Olivia she just had a cold. Olivia turned pale with anger and shouted, "Bitch, if you don't call the doctor right now, I'm going to kill you. Don't you

realize I'm hooked and so is this baby?" The doctor ordered morphine immediately, the baby stopped crying, her nose stopped running, and there weren't any more convulsions. It took months to
wean the baby from morphine. She's doing all right now, a pretty
child, but she's very hyper, has to keep moving all of the time.

The barbershop was quiet the morning I saw Olivia come out of
the bathroom with her cheeks flushed red from the rush of heroin
she'd just fixed. A few minutes later a customer went to the bathroom and came out complaining about the syringe and toilet paper
that wouldn't flush. Pancho, the owner, turned from his customer to
give Olivia an exasperated look, and she avoided his eyes. She was
wearing cutoff Levis and a white, man's T-shirt. Her hair had been
cut short in jail. She had trouble buttoning the jeans, but this
happens every time she does time . . . too much food, too much
time on her hands.

She was pacing up and down and couldn't sit still. Olivia was
madder than hell over her last bust—and that it took so long to get
her out on bond. She wanted to talk about it, and we wanted to hear
her story, but you don't ask. In her own good time she will tell us her
version of what happened. I'm sure it will be different from what the
cop who made the bust would say.

Four or five times she went to stand in the doorway, looking for
dates to pay for the fix she'd be needing in an hour or two. There was
a lull after the last customer, and she turned to me and started
talking about Angel. He is one of Olivia's connections for heroin
and cocaine. She said that Angel was going to testify against her to save
his own ass. Then she asked if I knew a narc by the name of Mike
Figueroa. He was a guy she had trusted, and she had even defended
him when the other addicts accused him of being the man.

✦ It really hurt my ego more than anything else, to think that this
guy could get so deep into my trust, that he could do this to me. At
first I thought he was a narc, I think it was about 1983, but he
convinced me he wasn't and he became a real, real good friend.

Hell, we used to fix together. I actually put the needle in his vein and shot him full of heroin. A narc won't let you do that, will he? I swear to God, he used to bring me stolen cars and I would take them to my connection in Nogales, Sonora, and sell them for four or five ounces of heroin and give it to him. It really hurts that I could have been so wrong. ✢

If it's true that Mike Figueroa is a cop and was doing the things Olivia has accused him of, he will eventually be removed from the department and he will be prosecuted. Cops always police their own and eliminate the weak links. The problem is there isn't any Mike Figueroa listed on the police department's personnel roster. Mike Figueroa is probably a street name. The man Olivia knew as Mike Figueroa, she said, was between five-nine and five-ten, medium build, big shoulders, like he works out. He had dark skin, hair down to his shoulders, kind of curly, and the last time she saw him he was wearing a Fu Manchu moustache. She said he was nice looking and she would have trusted him before she trusted any of us. Whoever he is, he plays the part very well.

Olivia left to take care of a date that honked and pulled around the corner, and Pancho mentioned he'd heard of this guy called Mike Figueroa.

Several guys, including Angel, the busted connection, have talked about this guy with the Fu Manchu and a big roll of money. He drives, by turns, a Ford Bronco, a white Thunderbird, and a maroon 1988 Mustang. He wears a lot of gold around his neck. He comes across as being a very successful drug dealer who likes to use a little shit himself sometimes. Olivia is angry, and rightfully so if the man she knew as Mike Figueroa was actually shooting drugs and stealing cars for her to sell. If he crossed the line, he'll end up doing some time. The question is, how much of Olivia's story can you believe? She's a three-time loser facing up to twenty-seven years on each of the three counts of possession and sale of narcotics, and fifteen years for conspiracy to sell stolen property. The indictment along with a prior conviction notification to the court could put her away for the rest of her life.

✤ It all started in April 1989, when I was hustling out of the Wagon Wheel Bar on the Sixth Avenue strip in South Tucson. Mike picked me up and took me to another bar and told me he wanted two papers of heroin and one of cocaine. That was cool with me, I figured he wanted to make a speedball. I went to Angel's to score for him and then I met him in the bar's parking lot. He was having a hard time finding his vein, so I fixed him with the coke and kept the two papers of heroin for later.

Six days later, he came after me again, and I scored two more papers. Then he told me he had a VCR that was still in the box and he wanted to see how much the connection would give him for it.

We went to Angel's house in Mike's car, and like a damn fool I took the VCR into Angel's house to find out how many papers we could get for it. It was a new machine, and Angel agreed to give me eighty bucks or four papers for it. I took the VCR back to where Mike was waiting, he told me he wanted the four papers, but he wanted to go with me. I told him, no deal. Then he wanted to go as far as the gate, telling me he didn't want to let the VCR out of his sight again. I allowed him to walk with me back to Angel's. We were standing by the gate when Angel came out and took the VCR from Mike and went back into the house. A few minutes later he came out with two papers of heroin and two of cocaine. He gave the papers to Mike—not to me but Mike. As far as I'm concerned, the deal was between them. We left, and after fixing up one paper each, he took the rest with him and let me off back at the bar. ✤

Four months after the incident with the VCR, Olivia was sitting at a bus stop in South Tucson. A police officer passed by, then made a U-turn and came back to serve a warrant on Olivia. He took her to the station house, and then after only a few minutes he loaded her back into the patrol car and took her downtown to the Tucson Police Department for a statement and booking.

The detectives who questioned Olivia were wasting their time and probably knew it. In the background through the two-way mirror on the interrogation room wall she could hear laughter that she recognized all too well. It was Mike. She knew that laugh and will never forget it. After the detectives handcuffed her for transport to county jail, they walked her past the water fountain in the hall. One of the detectives held the button for her while she took a drink. When she raised her head, she looked into the eyes of a startled Mike Figueroa. He dropped his eyes to his shoes.

Across the street from the barbershop, one of the new prostitutes on the avenue looked around and stepped down into a beige Mercury Cougar with a man we all knew as a narc. Olivia shook her head and said she'd warned the others about the new girl. They didn't believe her. And why should they?

Olivia says she was set up by a narc who fixes and fences. Angel swears in his statement to police that his deal was with Olivia and that he doesn't know a narc named Mike. If there is a Mike Figueroa, whether he's a good cop or a bad one, he'll have another version. And I just keep wondering, what really happened?

The Killer Narc

There are good cops, and once in a long while there is a bad cop. Most of the police officers I've worked with are good people. Some cops have financial and domestic problems just like everyone else, but they handle it, they take care of it, and don't bring it to work with them. But sometimes it happens. In Los Angeles in 1989, the L.A. County Sheriff discovered that he had an entire squad of narcotics agents who were on the take and probably selling the same drugs they took from the dealers they were busting. The same year a United States Customs agent was arrested for accepting bribes and for looking the other way when large shipments of drugs came through his station. I could go on and on, but yet, for every bad cop there are a thousand good cops.

I was talking to my old partner, John Lyons, about this. He retired from the Sheriff's Department as a major and now works for the probation department. "If you want to talk to a good cop, go talk to Pete Pershing," he told me. He paid Pete Pershing the highest compliment you can give a police officer: "Pete was a damn good street cop." So I went looking for him and, to my surprise, found him stuck behind a desk, working as an investigator for the Arizona Industrial Commission.

♣ I was a Vietnam veteran and was lucky enough to come back in one piece, without a lot of the character flaws or the mental instability of some of the returning vets. It was the era of Woodstock. These guys coming back from war were not necessarily drug addicts, just sort of lost for a time. They were the guys wandering around with the long hair, worn out, washed out, with a don't-give-a-shit attitude that many of us still can't understand. Most of them smoked a little pot and maybe did some acid, but eventually they turned out to be productive members of society.

That time passed and we survived, but I can see signs that it's coming back now, and it's going to come back worse. I saw it go from peace, love, and flowers to guns, greed, and death. It's getting more and more dangerous to work the streets, even more than it was in my time, and that was bad enough.

The drug scene of my era was not the same. The prices have changed and the drugs have changed. Now the agent has to deal with a deadly form of cocaine—crack. Heroin came in during the time I call the "Janis Joplin era," because she was heavy into booze and dope. I'm not blaming her for drugs in the United States, but her songs were laced with drugs and booze. I was already working under cover during this time, and so I was involved with these people, much more than your beat cop or even the detectives. Heroin was starting to be accepted in the middle-class community, something we had never seen here before. Then, when the hippies became yuppies, they started finding out that heroin was not all that great, that they could get strung out on it and possibly ruin their lives. That's when cocaine started getting popular.

Cocaine was being sold under the pretext that it was nonaddictive, it wouldn't hurt you, that it was socially acceptable. Heroin was considered a dirty habit, and the needles, syringes, and the cooking spoons were not really socially acceptable. Besides, the word was out that you could get all kinds of diseases from needles including hepatitis and god-knows-what. When coke came along, it was viewed as clean. You could snort it, and you weren't sticking needles in your veins. Coke was selling for forty dollars a gram or ten dollars a paper. Today it's more than twice that.

A lid of marijuana in the 1970s was ten dollars, that was one full ounce. I wouldn't buy it unless it covered four full fingers, and so naturally we called it a four-finger lid. A quarter ounce now brings thirty dollars.

In the 1970s tons of marijuana came over the Mexican border. Then we started hearing that a lot of the pot on the street was being grown locally. Why play beat-the-border when you can grow it? We have the climate for growing pot, and I found elaborate indoor systems with timed growing lights and irrigation systems so the grower wouldn't have to be out there cultivating and risk being seen and arrested. I'm telling you they grew some nice stuff. We confiscated some beautiful plants grown in backyards in some of the better neighborhoods right in town.

The psychedelics were all coming out of California. There were also some labs here in Tucson that manufactured methamphetamines. Speed was big during that era.

It was difficult for us to penetrate these labs. You almost need a chemistry background. You can't bust a speed lab until the drug reaches a certain stage in the process. We had to wait until they had a finished product. So we had to have an agent in the lab right at the time it was in its last stage. If we didn't time it just right, the only person we could get was the cooker. The cooker is following a recipe that was left there for him, and he doesn't deal with anyone except by phone. You have to be there when the main guy comes for the finished product, or all he loses is a cooker and the product. Thank goodness this fad phased out at that time and the users got wise to the harm speed could do.

Cocaine has really taken over. The first busts we made were small compared to what you read about now. I think my biggest buys were maybe five ounces. I did make quite a few buys eventually, but the coke dealers were very paranoid and hard to get to. The heroin dealer, as long as he had his fix, was not what I would call a dangerous or aggressive individual. The cocaine dealer was; he would snort his coke and then he'd start getting paranoid, thinking that everyone was watching him. This created new problems and started a new era in law enforcement. ✦

Sometimes cops have to kill the bad guys, that's why they carry guns. Police officers have to protect the public, and in doing so situations occur that require extreme measures and people die. In order to prevent having cops going around killing indiscriminately, police departments conduct extensive investigations every time a cop pulls the trigger. That's just the way it is, but I'll wager they don't have to put up with half the abuse that Pete Pershing did. Audie Murphy killed some 240 Germans—and received the Congressional Medal of Honor. Pete Pershing killed two criminals who tried to kill him in the act of committing felonies—and the press labeled him the "Killer Narc." If you think it isn't a war out there on our streets, you have another thought coming.

Pete Pershing's war is over. All he can do is sit back and read the press releases about the drugs and the killings. It isn't his problem anymore. That's not the way he wanted it, but it happened, and the drug dealers in Tucson are better off for it.

✦ My thinking is that too often departments worry too much about publicity, and this affects the way they think. You see, they don't seem to realize that out there on the streets you need to have a man under cover for two years before he's really good and you can start feeling comfortable with him. It seems that administrators become afraid that if a man has been out too long, he might slip to the criminals' side. There's no way he would, but just when he starts knowing what's expected of him, they take him out and put a new guy in his place. This makes the job twice as dangerous for the rest of us because it's hard working with a new partner. When I had a partner for a year or two, I felt safer with him than with anyone. You were your partner's best friend because your life was in his hands. Let me give you an example: If we went into a house where they were selling heroin and they separated us, which they often do, and they were asking him certain questions and me the same questions, I'd know exactly what to answer, and so would he. If I had a new partner, it would be scary, real scary. My first shooting was because of that. I had a new partner and we were going to make a buy, some heroin. I couldn't take him in with me because my contact didn't want me to.

I was Anglo, he was Mexican, but they didn't know him and didn't trust him. He was afraid to go in there anyway because one of the main people selling was a woman, and he knew her. He had just come to us from being a school-resources officer, and her daughter or son had been in trouble in school. He had been involved with the case and was afraid she would recognize him.

I couldn't stall this buy. I had been waiting months to get into this place, and this guy tells me, "Come on, you want to score a gram of heroin, I'll take you in." So I go in with him. My partner has to sit in the car a block away and see how I make out. Right away I can see I'm in a bad situation because they want me to fix with them. That happens quite often, but if you're experienced, you can usually talk your way out of it. This was one time I couldn't. I had four or five defendants in the house, all Mexican, and they want me to fix heroin with them.

I was setting up to buy another ounce that night from a guy called Lichi, who was bad news. He was supposed to be a counselor at the new heroin-addiction clinic called the Hope Center, where they dispense methadone to drug addicts so they won't have to be out committing crimes to buy drugs. Although he was officially a counselor, he was still dealing dope through his girlfriend, and we knew it. I wanted him bad. I was going to buy and walk on a gram and then come back later that night and negotiate with him on an ounce, then bust him on that. But I couldn't get out of there, they wanted me to fix and they weren't going to let me out until I did. They already had a needle and syringe out on the kitchen table. I told them I had a new rig and would use my own.

In those days I used to change the places where I carried my gun, and this time it was inside my boot. Not the best place in the world to carry it because you can't get to it in a hurry, but I preferred it to my jockstrap. Working under cover you learn that your gun isn't your best defense, nor is your badge. It's your wits. That's what a lot of guys can't handle when they have to work under cover. They don't have that badge they are used to having to protect them. Most of the time you can't even have your gun with you. If you carry a gun, you better not carry one that looks like a cop's gun. Anyway, I told them I had my rig in my boot and I always used my own outfit. I knew I was in a pickle because if I didn't fix, they were going to put me down and fix me themselves, and nobody's putting that shit in my body. I had already made up my mind that Lichi would have to wait for another day. So I took the gun out and turned to the side so I'd have the kitchen wall to my back and told them I was a narcotics officer and they were all under arrest.

The guy who took me into the house was Roman Helton, and as

soon as I told them I was a narc he freaked out. So I had four people in there, two women and two men. I got the two men on the floor and had them drop their pants, 'cause you aren't going to run very fast with your pants around your ankles. I put the women back to back in chairs and tied them together with a belt. I had some coat hangers and put them around the one guy's hands and twisted them to hold him. What I was going to do was tie them up and go out and yell to my partner to get on the radio and send a uniformed unit to give me some help. About that time Roman Helton jumped up and ran out the front door. I ran out the back to cut him off. We met at the side yard and right away started wrestling. We went around and around and around, making a big commotion. I knew he'd been in prison before, he had priors for bank robbery and other things, but he was just freaked because all this time he'd been selling to a cop and he'd taken a cop into somebody's house who was a big dealer. He was going to look like a snitch and he probably thought if he caught time, they would kill him in prison.

He had me by the wrist of my gun hand, and as we struggled, he would sometimes have it pointing at me, I would turn it back toward him, and in the struggle for the gun it went off and hit him in the stomach.

I ran back inside to cover the other people and wait for my backup. Shortly after that there were police cars all over the place, and a big crowd gathered in front of the house. The uniform cops did a smart thing. They handcuffed me and took me out as if I was one of the suspects. They took me down to TPD and left me in a room with handcuffs on for over an hour, which I didn't appreciate and still don't understand. At this time my only concern was how Roman was doing. You don't ever want to hurt anybody, never. Finally one of the detectives, who had quite a bit of experience on the force and knew what I was going through, came in and told me Roman had died.

They were going to take a statement from me, and that was OK. I expected that, but then I overheard some of the brass talking, and it seemed that all they were worried about was the press release. How was it going to look for the department? An undercover narcotics officer had shot and killed a man during a narcotics buy, and all they wanted to know was what kind of dope it was. If a suspect had been shot and killed over a marijuana buy, it might look bad. When they were told it was a heroin buy, I could hear a sigh of relief. A heroin buy was OK. It didn't matter to me which one it was, I didn't make the man die, he made himself die, but I felt terrible about it. I do to this day, but all they cared about was public opinion. Killing a suspect in a heroin bust was OK, everybody hates heroin. That's when I started to realize who and what I was working for. If I hadn't actually seen and heard the reaction of my superiors, I wouldn't have believed it. If someone else had told me my bosses didn't give a damn about Pete Pershing, I wouldn't have believed them.

I was back on the street in four days. Internal Affairs checked it out and the department cleared me, it was a justifiable kill. I would still be on the streets today if they had let me, but the brass eventually decided I was hot. I would have stayed because I really liked what I was doing and I really felt I was doing something effective.

You know, some cops find their home right away, whether it's homicide or burglary or working uniform on the graveyard shift. Some never do. I had found mine. But the brass think you've been there too long, you're hot, and they pull you out even though I proved to them you never get too hot in narcotics. You change your appearance all of the time and you can change locations to the different groups that are dealing. You switch to another end of town, change identification, switch cars, and you're back on the street again, just as effective as you were before. You have to use a little ingenuity. When one well goes dry, you just look around.

A good cop can look at someone and know right away if they're holding, if they're users or dealers or even if they can score for you from somebody else. It's not entrapment to walk up to some guy and ask him if he knows where you can score a paper. If I ask you that, you're going to tell me to go to the newsstand. But if you're a doper, you know what I'm talking about. You already have the seed in your mind, I didn't plant it there, so legally that's not entrapment. Maybe I see a guy on a corner, and three or four people hit on him and walk off. Right away I know what he is and then I hit on him. You make buys from as many of his associates as you can and then arrest all of them together. You spread fear and paranoia around them and lower their survival rate.

That's the specific purpose of mass arrests—to spread fear and paranoia among the dealers and users. Make them think long and hard before they sell to anyone, make them want to stay within their own circle of friends and not branch out. But when you do this, you increase the chances of violent retaliation by the dealers. Somebody has to pay. The dealer might not know who made the buy that busts him, who the narc is, but in his paranoia he doesn't care, he just lashes out. I don't think there are that many police officers on the street today buying street dope. And I think it's a shame. I don't say this boastfully or resentfully, but I just don't think they know how to do it anymore. What the department did was take all of the experienced guys and wash them out of there and throw all these other guys into the narcotics division. They know how to do remote-control narcotics, surveillance, snitches, the setup deals. What I mean is they don't know how to get out in the street and score some stuff. There's a few who might do it hit-and-miss, and they get lucky sometimes, but I mean to do an effective job day in and day out.

They need four or five guys who are willing to do it like we did. We had to work long hours and we had to vary our hours, not just from nine to five. I was married during this era, and I must say my wife was very understanding, but it's difficult. Some marriages survived and some didn't. Some of my partners had trouble at home, and that puts all of us under more pressure. I don't blame the wives. After all, your husband looks like a creep, he talks like one, and he has to act like one out on the street. You have to be able to turn that switch off and on. When you go to work, you have to put on your act, and when you go home, turn it off and go back to being normal. Some guys can't do that.

Not only that, but you have to think like a drug dealer and an addict, get down to their level in order to be effective. Some guys can and some can't. We had some guys tell us they could never think like that. We always told them we weren't asking them to live like that. We wanted them to keep their same morals and ideals, but there are people who live and think this way, and when you're out there with them, you have to understand how they think in order to know how things work in the street. Some guys could not do it. They think it's a step down, when it really isn't. You know, as cops we're not any better or any worse than anyone else. In my era you couldn't go out there smelling nice with clean clothes every day. I used to wear the dirtiest, nastiest crap I could find and go without taking a bath for a day or two if that's what it took. If you go into a drug house and are wearing the right clothes and you act and you look and you talk right, but you smell like big daddy, they become suspicious right away. A dope addict doesn't usually care about his person anyway, he doesn't care if his laundry is clean, if his teeth are brushed every day and things like that.

Some guys just couldn't lower themselves to that level. Like I couldn't stand working vice and prostitution. I could buy dope but not women. They put me there for three weeks one time and I asked out of it, couldn't handle it, it used to make my skin crawl. But one of the guys I work with now used to work vice and had a great time of it. Now with age and what I've gone through, you couldn't get me near dope and needles. I guess it's because we used to get stuck a lot with needles. Sometimes we'd arrest a guy because we couldn't get out of there. They wanted you to fix or something like that, and all you could do was arrest them. They would sometimes go into a rage and get the syringe and needle and stab you with it. Then you had to go to the hospital and get a shot for hepatitis. Let me tell you, we hated it because there's nothing worse than a narc coming down with something like hepatitis. It made you look like you were using.

So you reported every scratch and needle stab you had. Sometimes, when you were serving a search warrant, you'd be running your hand along an edge and hit a needle, and you better run down and get a shot right away. Today, what do you take for AIDS? I don't know. Sometimes that needle is just as bad as holding a gun on you.

I've seen so-called "buddies" in our department turn on us. They go out and arrest some guy and he'll tell them, yeah, I know that cop, I used to fix with him all the time, and they believe him. Then we were either in Internal Affairs taking a polygraph test or at the clinic giving a urine sample. You get to the point where you're spending more time defending yourself than you are being effective. There will always be somebody who will misuse the system, the rotten apple in the barrel, and it rubs off on the rest of the guys. When we went in on a big pot bust in my era and we found over $3,000 in cash, we called the Internal Revenue Service immediately. Sometimes you'd go into a bedroom and there were several grocery bags on the floor full of hundred-dollar bills. You ask them who this belongs to. They don't know, never seen it before you walked in. Thousands of dollars just lying there that don't belong to anyone. You got cops who were making four or five hundred dollars a month with three kids at home. They could reach in and grab a couple of bundles and nobody would know the difference. I never saw that happen. I've worked with guys who were having serious financial problems, who had the chance but wouldn't touch a penny of it.

My era was free love and peace, the hippie generation, a bunch of kids who were falling into hard drugs with the old established dealers. Pot didn't seem to satisfy them any longer, which was too bad because I always felt we wasted a lot of law enforcement time and money on marijuana when it wasn't as bad as the hallucinogens and the hard stuff. We spent too much time on marijuana that didn't cause an addiction. I know, there are two types of addiction, psychological and physical, but what I'm saying is we needed to concentrate on the hard drugs, heroin and cocaine, and certainly all of the hallucinogens, the chemicals. I have never seen anyone die from an overdose of marijuana. If somebody wants to show me one, I'll learn something. I'm not advocating its legalization, but I've never seen a guy go out and habitually commit burglaries or armed robberies to support a "marijuana habit." Maybe the answer is to decriminalize the possession of one ounce of pot like Oregon did as far back as my era. The drug dealer is going to deal anything he can make a profit on, whether it's pot or cocaine. The old reasoning was that anyone who uses pot will go on to hard drugs, and anyone who deals pot will go on to dealing heroin or cocaine. That's not necessarily true. I hate to blow that bubble, but that is not true. ♣

The Metropolitan Area Narcotics Squad, better known as the Metro Unit, was a federally funded police activity designed to take the local dope dealer off the street, using police officers instead of informers to make controlled buys. It had been tried in Tucson before the grant was approved by putting a couple of undercover police officers on the street, and it met with some success. It was new and dangerous, and there was a lot to learn, but it did one important thing. It brought city and county law enforcement together as one unit. The Tucson Police Department was the administrator of the grant. The assignment was to buy street narcotics, working on the theory that the local cops knew the local people.

The hometown cop could go in, make his buy, walk on it, make another buy, and keep doing this until he was able to penetrate deeper and deeper into the drug culture while accumulating warrants for one big frenzy of arrests that would create fear and paranoia in local drug circles. The idea was to take the street dealer off the street and so reduce the number of addicts who were out there burglarizing homes, shoplifting, and committing armed robberies to support their habits. It cost the cop ten dollars to buy a paper of heroin. For twenty dollars you could put a street dealer away for five years.

Two or three years after the Metro Unit was started, the agency known then as the Bureau of Narcotics saw how effective the Metro Unit was becoming and realized that there was a lot of drug activity in Tucson. They opened an office here. The structure agreed upon was that the BNDD would work the high-level violators, the Arizona Department of Public Safety would work some street drugs but mostly the intermittent violators, and the Metro Unit would continue to deal with the street dealers and addicts. Pete Pershing was part of the Metro Unit.

♦ I looked pretty bad in the 1970s. I had hair down to my waist and a beard. I looked and acted like a hippie. We would pick up information from one addict who would lead us to another, and he would take us in to someone else and so forth. I generally didn't look like I was the type to have a large amount of money to be buying large quantities of narcotics, but if my partner and I could penetrate deep enough to meet someone with a large supply, we told him we knew a person who did have the money and was looking to make a big buy. If the dealer sounded interested, we would usually bring in a federal or state agent. The large cases are dangerous because they usually end up in a bust. You make the buy, there are large amounts of money on the table, lots of guns, and there is always the threat of a rip-off. They don't know you're a cop, and they may try to rip you off. The street buys were harder to make because you had to convince the individual that you were in fact a user.

This brought, and I'll tell you this honestly, a lot of discredit from our fellow police officers and the citizens in this community. A police officer who had hair down to his waist, had simulated track marks on his arms, which he put there himself, had a dirt-bag way of handling himself, and talked street lingo fluently was really looked down upon. I think those of us who worked under cover took the brunt of abuse from our own police agencies and the public because we looked as bad as the guys we were buying from. Every time we went to court, the defendant would be shaved, looking clean, and we'd look terrible. Of course, the defense would go after the police officer, making him look even worse than the defendant to the jury.

Our job was to get as many buys as possible from a street dealer. If we could, we would get two or three buys for twenty dollars a paper from a dealer, then testify before a grand jury and have a warrant issued. The detectives would go out and pick up the dealer, arrest him, and have him indicted. The dealer would never know which sale busted him. He knew he had made several sales on or about that day, but which one had been the cop? What the county attorney would usually do is plea-bargain him down to one count and send him up for three to five, and he'd never see the man who busted him. I was able to work under cover effectively for almost six years. I could go to one part of town and buy from Yaqui Indians and then go to a different part of town and buy from the Mexican dealers in the barrios, or maybe go to the downtown area around Sabino Alley and buy from the black dealers.

When I joined the Metro Unit, the older heads told me there was no way a *gavacho* [Anglo, white boy] could ever buy from the Yaqui and Mexican dealers who traditionally control most of the heroin in Tucson. That was part of our history. As far as the west and south sides of town, those people have been selling heroin and marijuana for eons and smuggling and fencing stolen property to sell across the border in Mexico. This has been going on forever. Hell, their grandparents and maybe even their great-grandparents were doing the same thing before them. They were harder to penetrate, to make that first buy, but once you got in, you could go back and buy as much as you wanted.

Now, when it came to the central part of town, you were getting away from traditional dope dealing. This is where the hippies and the flower children were hanging out, doing their grass and angel dust and using all kinds of uppers and downers and hallucinogens. Himmel Park and Speedway Boulevard in the early 1970s was just an open-air drug market. You could pick up anyone hitchhiking on

Speedway, and by the time you got to Himmel Park where they were going to sell their dope, they would have tried to sell you at least a lid of pot. There were a lot of chemicals on the street too. Himmel Park was so wide open that people were cooking and fixing right out in the open, right out on the hoods of their cars. Himmel Park is in a very nice neighborhood, no slum area by a long shot. What we had here was the spread of what I call the bad drugs, the hard drugs like heroin, from the lower economic community into the middle-class community.

There were some young white guys who had good connections and could go into South Tucson and buy heroin. Let's call one of them Clyde. Clyde could go to the South Side with fifty dollars and buy five papers. These papers were approximately two hundred milligrams of good heroin. Clyde would cut the papers three times and bring them back to Himmel Park and sell them. That way he could support his habit and still double his money. We felt that even though he was just a street dealer, he was still worth our time. After all, he was making money and, even worse, he was spreading heroin addiction to another portion of the community. We had kids coming from the east side and north side to Himmel Park to buy pot and LSD, and now heroin was being introduced to them. Normally these kids wouldn't have gone to the South Side or over to Yaqui Village to buy drugs, couldn't have if they had wanted to. But now it was becoming available to them on their own turf, and the addiction started spreading. Then, all of a sudden, our burglary rate went sky-high too.

Himmel Park was becoming a dangerous place to work undercover narcotics and make buys. We had two agents caught up in an altercation there, and one of them was shot in the hand. The department was afraid of approaching it again for a while, but we convinced them to let us back in and we started making buys again. Only this time we had officers in a church steeple nearby with binoculars to watch the buys and then radio a uniform car to go in and make the arrest. The defendant wouldn't know which long-hair turned him in, because in a matter of fifteen minutes he had already made five or six sales.

We were starting to spread that fear and paranoia again, and by then we had some officers who had been in deep cover for two years, who were becoming very effective. We were learning how to handle ourselves, how to be on the defensive when making a buy so we could get out of there without any trouble and without having to arrest the guy. A lot of times they wanted you to fix with them, and that's something we could not do. So you had to make up excuses, and they had to be legitimate ones to make a buy and not fix or be fixed by them. It was hard, but once you made one buy and the other dealers saw it, they trusted you. Then you could go in and make as many buys as you needed before arresting a whole bunch of them at once. That way, when we came back with indictments, we could wipe out an entire dealing section at one time.

Again, we had to get so close to the dealers and the addicts in order to make our buys that even some of our fellow officers distrusted us and probably felt we had crossed over that line. Any time you work undercover narcotics or vice you can assume that your credibility is not going to be the same as it was before. I don't care how clean you are. Everyone thinks that once you've been in the dirt, you must have got dirt on you, which is not true.

Most of the fellows I worked narcotics with have not done well as far as their police careers are concerned after going under cover. I think that's really one of the biggest injustices of the whole thing. The undercover detective is in a no-man's-land, between the department and between the street, never truly accepted by either one.

It's been my experience that very few turn out bad. But there was a case in our department about twenty years ago where two officers crossed that line. Again the department handled it badly. The two officers were minorities, and the brass didn't want the publicity, so the officers were dismissed and not prosecuted. They should have been. We weeded out our own in narcotics, washed our own laundry, so to speak. Even if we had a guy under cover who wasn't dirty, wasn't really doing anything wrong, but he was going out drinking in bars instead of being in the street making buys, or if he was chasing women, hey, we'd go to the sergeant and tell him the guy wasn't working out, let's get him out of here.

The job isn't for everyone. It's a tough job because you're left out of everything. You can't socialize with your friends on the department, you cannot associate with them, and you know how police officers are. We hang around with our own kind because they're the only ones we trust. You can't go to the shopping mall with your family because some guy from the street might see you. How are you going to explain the wife and kids? You really isolate yourself from the rest of the straight world. You almost have to eat and breathe the drug world and think only of the drug world.

In the era before I went to work in narcotics, the officers had much greater freedom and latitude. We were fairly regimented, but I found out that no matter how many checks and balances you have for the undercover officer, you can't control everything. You have to find an individual with a lot of self-control, strict self-discipline, and the attitude of wanting to do the job the right way.

Sometimes you get separated from your partner and he has to wait for you down the block and use his instincts about how far to let you go before coming after you. It gets damn dangerous when a dealer separates you and your partner. For instance, I went to this house with a black guy who I had already made two or three buys from but who we hadn't indicted yet. We were going to let him run for a while to see what it would lead to. The guy took me to this house in the black section of town but wouldn't let my partner go in with us. He didn't trust him. When I walked in the door, my partner was two blocks away and I was the only white boy in the place. The first thing that happened when I went into the room was they threw me up against the wall with a gun to my back and took all of my clothes off and searched me. The reason for this was to see if I had a gun on me and to make sure I wasn't the man. I couldn't believe it; inside the house were a bunch of guns that had been reported stolen in a burglary in Phoenix three days before. I scored my heroin and got out of there in a hurry. That night the detectives hit the house with a search warrant and recovered all of the guns and arrested everyone in the house.

My feelings when they threw me up against the wall were of complete fear. If you're not afraid, you're approaching complete stupidity and you're going to get yourself or somebody else killed. But you have to make them feel that you're not really deathly afraid of them, that this is all routine. To show too much fear would be a big mistake. Indignation is acceptable and expected. For instance, I was working the Yaqui Village and the South Side where the Yaqui and Mexican dealers are pretty damn tough. They were constantly checking me out, and it was mostly because I was from a different culture and my skin was a different color. I'm not saying this was a racial thing, but there are racial barriers in this world and you have to face up to it. They were always accusing me of being the man, and I had to appear to be insulted at being thought of as a snitch or a cop. I had to be aggressive. Sometimes I had to pull my knife on them to prove I wasn't what they were accusing me of. We lived with the possibility of getting cut, stabbed, or even tortured and shot in the back of the head, execution style.

Being aggressive worked for me once on the South Side. I was working the Ozark Bar on South Sixth Avenue when this tough-looking *vato* [guy], as they called themselves, comes up to me and accuses me of being a narc. I pulled my knife and threw him up against the wall in the bathroom and scared the shit out of him, to the point he respected me from then on. He was holding, he was selling, but he didn't want to sell to this white boy with the long hair who might be a narc. He wanted to see how much sand I had. Then after that they'd sell to you, they figured you'd been around and knew what was coming down.

The Ozark is gone now, having made way for the South Tucson City Hall and administrative buildings, but in its heyday it was *the* dealing place on the South Side. This was where a lot of the more open dealing went on. There were prostitutes in there who were also users, and then there were good everyday people too. You had to know who was who. A guy would be shooting pool and he'd see someone who he knew was looking to buy, and just by using eye contact and body language he'd meet him in the bathroom and sell to him. These were the small-time dealers who were selling the 200-milligram papers that they'd already cut twice.

There were other places, of course, but the hottest places were the Yaqui Indian villages, with the one on the northwest side being the worst. There were families living there who had been selling narcotics for three generations. The Suarezes and the Romeros were two that come to mind. In back of the Romeros' was the "death house," so called because a couple of them had died there from an overdose of heroin. That's where they kept their needles and outfits. If you wanted to score, you went to the house in front, and if you wanted to fix, you went to the death house.

In those days the addicts fixed with needles that looked like fishhooks, and everybody used them over and over. That's probably changed with the fear of AIDS now, but then you have guys using heroin who don't really care about themselves anyway. These are the old-time users. The young user today is different, more aware and more careful. Heroin and cocaine are a death wish. I look back, and a lot of the people I used to make buys from are dead now, most of them victims of their own greed for another fix, a bigger high. Sooner or later the dope will catch up with them, or just what's going on out there will. It always seemed to me that the users in the barrios and Indian villages could handle it better because they came from a culture where dope was a way of life. The people either used it, or they didn't. Most people didn't, but it was more acceptable with them. People in the barrio mind their own business. They feel if you want to kill yourself with drugs, that's up to you, as long as you don't bother them.

Some of the Mexican and Yaqui addicts we encountered had the entire family involved in drugs. The father knew the kids used dope, probably was a user or former user himself, the mother either used or sold dope and served as the mule for bringing dope across the border in her vagina at one time or another. I know that sounds cruel and harsh, or even racist, but it was the truth. They were all involved in it one way or another. That was, and I guess in some cases still is, the family business.

When drugs left the barrio and spread into the middle class and even to the rich white folks, you had a different type of addict. For one thing, there was no acceptance by the rest of the family like there was in the barrio. I busted a college student for sale and possession. His father owned a trucking business in the Midwest. The kid sort of fell into the drug scene with the rest of his crowd because it was the in thing to do. After I busted him, he fixed up one more time. He got hold of some bad stuff and also hit a nerve. For a long time he lost the feeling in his arms. He stills keeps in touch with his attorney and even asked to see me once. I knew he was rehabilitated and working with his dad, so I agreed to see him. He told me I had done him a favor by arresting him, and I think I did. I know most of the people we busted wouldn't agree, but sometimes we did do them a favor.

The big dealers were all Mexican. They had names like Chavetas, Lichi, Gato, and Pingas. Then there were Indians, Joe Ybarra and Chile Verde, who were pretty active too. Arnulfo Cordova was the one called Pingas. He was the big guy, and so was Peter Lopez Valenzuela, known as Gato. We got most of them, and they caught some prison time, but I see where some are out now and back in business. Pingas was big time, and he sticks in my mind because he used race horses as his front, racing several horses in Arizona and also in California. That gave him the perfect excuse to be traveling between Tucson and California. Most of the heroin he smuggled in from Mexico went straight to Los Angeles. The heroin was transported in the horse trailers and vans, hidden in with the tack and in the trailers themselves. It was a front that nobody in those days would think to look at. It looked clean, it was away from what they now call the drug profile. Some of it went to his bagmen in Tucson, but the bulk of it went to L.A. for distribution. If it hadn't been for his greed, Pingas might have stayed out of jail for a lot longer. But he got greedy, and I made three ten-dollar buys from him myself. The big guys make mistakes too. Don't tell me the big guys don't sell out the back door. Sometimes I think it's not the money so much as the thrill of the deal; the danger involved pumps up the old adrenaline or something.

Not everyone who makes money from drugs is a smuggler or a dealer. We had shops in Tucson that were building smuggling cars. There was one I recall at the corner of Sixth and Santa Rita. Their specialty were Volkswagens and Volkswagen vans. Eventually they got a hot profile, but they were good. They could do a Volkswagen bug where you could carry about five hundred pounds of pot inside the door panels, hollowed out with compartments in them that were almost impossible to detect. Ironically, the business was called the Poor Boy's Automotive Garage.

Pot's a bust because it's bulky, it smells, and it's easy for the police to get probable cause to search you. With cocaine and heroin you smuggle in a lot of money's worth of the drug in a very small container. We had a lot of college kids who would come out here and decide to take home a couple of kilos of pot with them for Christmas to sell to their friends in New Jersey or New York or wherever they might be from. So these kids were playing dope dealers, trying to double their money while visiting their folks. Marijuana was selling for fifty to eighty dollars a pound, that was tops. So they would find a dealer to sell them a few pounds, put it in their luggage and check it in at the airport. Well, the feds finally got wind of this and started using profile checks and dogs to sniff the luggage. The kids used all kinds of ingenious ways to cover up the odor, all the way from mothballs to redwood chips. You name it, they tried it.

This was a different kind of dealer with different motives—just a college kid trying to make a little extra spending money over the holidays. Mom and dad were shocked when we arrested them. They would sometimes buy a steamer trunk, which can hold from fifty to a hundred pounds of pot, and check it through to Hometown U.S.A. This was a large amount of pot for them, so what we would do is get a search warrant, search the trunk and get a sample of the pot, and keep that here for evidence. Then we called the authority on the other end and let them know what was coming. We let the defendant go on thinking he was doing all right. The cops on the other end watched him as he picked up his luggage and followed him until he started to make his distribution. Then they arrested him and as many others as they could pull in. This was something new in undercover narcotics—the cops were working together for a change.

It hasn't always been that way. Every department wanted to have its own special unit and all the glory. Consequently the units were always overlapping and doing the job over again. To have the Pima County Attorney's Narcotic Strike Force, the Metropolitan Area Narcotics Unit, the Arizona Department of Public Safety, and the Drug Enforcement Agency all working the same thing was kind of dumb.

When the Tucson Metro Unit was started, there were only two officers from the police department, Perry Lowe and Tommy Gomez. Then Gene Anaya came in, and Orville Ridgley was the sergeant. Bob Gibson came over from the Sheriff's Department and got himself shot five times during a bust. Then George Corty got it in a shoot-out at Himmel Park, hit in the hand. We had a lot of guys hurt at first because we didn't really know what we were doing. A lot of those early situations where we had officers shot were not stupidity; they lost control of the buy. Like following a guy out into the desert to look at his stash of marijuana when all of the time they knew you're a narc and they were going to execute you right on the spot. That's what happened to Bob, and it's a wonder he's alive today. And this was just over a couple of small sales. There's no doubt they were going to execute him. They had him get out of the car and told him to kneel down with his hands behind his head. Bob wasn't about to get shot in that position without a fight, so he made a try for it and

they shot him five times. Left him there to die like a dog. But he
survived. He wouldn't have if he had gone down on his knees to
them. After that we called him Bullet Bob. A few years later he
became a justice of the peace, a job he holds to this day.

We had a lot of cowboys come into the Metro Unit who wanted to
get into dope because they thought it was going to be a lot of fun
arresting people and pulling guns and being in hot-car chases like
they used to see in the movies. Then they found out that's not what it
was. It's not a very glamorous assignment. Some people it fits real
good . . . others it doesn't.

The bottom line is: I was involved in two shootings that resulted in
the death of two men. I was accused along the way of being Wyatt
Earp or, as the local press called me in headlines, the "Killer Narc."
There, toward the end of my time with the Metro Unit, we pulled a
lot of what we called roundups where we put the undercover agents
in the back seat of a patrol car wearing those yellow raincoats,
called slickers, and black ski masks. Our detectives would go into
the house and bring out two or three guys or as many as were in
there, and the detective would point at one of the suspects. If he was
the one we made the buy from and had an indictment for, we'd give
a thumbs-up signal. If not, the thumbs down. The detective would
go right down the line and arrest as many as we had buys from. And
that's where the papers got the title for an article, "The Unmasking
of the Killer Narc." Naturally I was the Killer Narc for them because
I had killed Roman Helton in that bust I told you about earlier.

We used to do that for paranoia. I mean, that scared the shit out
of them. But it wasn't force or police brutality or anything like that.
Just the paranoia factor. They never knew when a narc in a mask was
going to come into their house and finger them up for sales they had
made earlier. Pretty scary, huh? But that's where they got that shit,
and newspeople always want to make it a bigger and better story.
Some people on the department were already giving me credit for
killing five people, and that wasn't true. Just Roman Helton when I
was with the police department, and a kid on the roof of a jewelry

store he was breaking into when I was with the Sheriff's Department, and that was while I was in uniform. It was one of those unfortunate things. I didn't want to shoot that kid at all. I almost got myself shot on that one because I actually waited too long. He had a gun and was bringing it around to shoot at me when I fired.

Cocaine, at the start of the 1970s, was advertised on the street as the nonaddictive drug for the new middle class, and that's bullshit. That stuff's bad. It's addictive as hell, it'll change your personality and even cost you your life. You know and I know that there were many kids involved with drugs who were the children of prominent people, but what is not widely known is that a lot of prominent people were what I call the "easy-chair dope dealers," and here I'm including attorneys as well as businessmen. I could never prove any judges being involved, although I have heard of some, but I know there were two attorneys here definitely involved. I could never get the people we busted to turn on them. These are the people I had to contend with, and as it turned out, I had to do it on my own.

What I went through after the second killing was bullshit too. I had quit the police department and transferred to the Sheriff's Department. TPD had put me on a desk for doing my job, and now it was happening again, only this time the Sheriff's Department put me on search and rescue, which is a good unit, but not for a street cop. This is not a boast, but when you're effective at doing something that causes a great deal of harm to a group of people who are doing something illegal but who have good legal connections, their reaction is to get even with you, get you off the street somewhere so you can't hurt them anymore. They turn a good thing bad, and the department is quick to believe it. They are scared to death of the press and won't stand up for you, so you have to have a little pride and take your pension after just thirteen years. Six hundred a month isn't bad, and I'm thankful for it, but I know guys on the department retiring with two thousand a month who sat on their asses for twenty years. That's not right either.

They found a way to get me off the street by labeling me the

Killer Narc. That was pretty effective. I think they did a real good job of doing that. I feel that the criminal element in Tucson won, and the city police department and the Sheriff's Department stuck their tails between their legs and walked away from me. I still, to this day, think that was wrong. Where were all the people who said they were on my side? Nobody was there for me, that's why I stay to myself even now. ✤

There wasn't enough time to get to know a man from one or two meetings that spanned only three, maybe four hours. That's how much time Pete Pershing allowed himself to try and make me understand what it meant to him to be an undercover cop. For years he's kept his feelings pretty much to himself, swallowing what was for him a bitter pill and what he considers a victory for the underworld of drugs. What hurts and haunts Pete Pershing is, in my opinion, that he feels that there was a great deal more he could have contributed, that he could still be accomplishing a lot in the battle against drugs. What hurts him most is that he believes that the people and the department he wanted most to belong to let him down when it counted.

The reporter who came up with the title "Killer Narc" had as much to do with removing Pershing from the street as the unfortunate circumstances that caused Pershing to kill two men in the line of duty. That reporter was doing his job the best way he knew how. He was trained to come up with a phrase that grabs the reader. Killer Narc is a grabber. Nothing personal, no real harm intended.

I remember a former dealer named Lichi telling me when I asked about Pete Pershing that he had been trying to find out who he was for a long time. Pershing was really a pain in the ass to drug dealers. Everybody said they knew who Pete Pershing was, had seen him face to face, but no one could describe him when it really counted. Before the shootings, there were people in the streets who would have paid big money to eliminate him.

At first I thought that maybe the law enforcement agencies he worked for had done him a great wrong. Then I heard something from two different, completely unrelated sources. One was a drug dealer and one was an ex-cop who had worked with Pete. The dealer told me: "We were hearing on the street that he was trigger-happy and had already shot some people. To watch out for him." The ex-cop was not a narc, but he did know Pete. "The things we were hearing in the department was that maybe Pete was stretched out too thin, that maybe he had been too quick in pulling the trigger, that the job was getting to him. Some people felt it was a good thing for him and for the department when they took him off the street. I don't ever remember anyone ever saying he was dirty, just that he needed time to sort himself out."

Getting transferred is part of the job, it happens to everyone who pins on the badge. If you're working one of the high-profile jobs like homicide or narcotics and you really like it, even if you're doing a great job, you have to accept the reality that some day you're going to have to move on to another detail. Street cops don't have a permanent home. Even paper cops get moved from time to time.

There are good cops like Pete, and there are bad cops like the compromised ones in Los Angeles. The bad cop has to be taken off the rolls and prosecuted to the limit. Sometimes a good cop has to be taken off the street. It does take a lot of soul-searching to say it's time to bring the undercover cop in. Given what I found out about Pete, and having met the man, I would have hated to be the one to make that determination. In the long run it was probably right for Pete and for the department. There were other areas where he could have contributed. He chose not to, he made the call, and he has to live with it.

6 GET OLD MAN LICHI

*I know I can stop, and I
will, because I don't want to
meet God as a dope fiend. I
can't look Him in the face if
I don't try.*

—Lichi

ORLD WAR II HAD BROUGHT US
closer together as a nation, but many of the soldiers who were
assigned to bases all over the country and those who served in other
parts of the world were no longer content to stay in one place, at
home, anymore. Many drug addicts and casual users from other
parts of the country had learned how easy it was to obtain and use
drugs in the Southwest and in the border towns of Mexico.

Enforcement was lax. The customs inspectors were more concerned about how much tequila and mescal you had in your shopping bag or whether you were bringing birds or fruit across than they
were about how much marijuana or opium you had in your pockets.
The large cities with run-down ghettos and barrios were the first to
feel the rise in crimes committed by addicts. Most of the larger
police departments reported that the crime rate had risen over
seventy-five percent as a result of drug abuse. Alarming as this
was, most of us didn't worry about drugs because it was the poor
and minorities who were doing them.

Until the early 1950s, heroin was not the drug of choice among
most addicts. They preferred opium. Marijuana was just starting to
become popular. Law-enforcement officials tended to deal with the
crimes the addict committed after the fact rather than eliminate the

cause. In 1956 the entire drug enforcement budget for the city of Los Angeles was $100,000 for the whole year, and this included the innovative "buy-program" money used to purchase drugs from dealers. The entire "buy" budget for the Pima County Sheriff's Department in Tucson was—one hundred dollars. The increasing flow of drugs into the United States through Mexico, Cuba, the Far East, and the Caribbean went unchecked. A new army of drug users was being created from coast to coast.

In the late 1960s, someone came up with the idea of taking the profit out of the hands of the drug dealers by creating methadone clinics all over the country. The theory being to give away methadone so the heavy drug users wouldn't have to rob, steal, and prostitute themselves to buy heroin. A mixture of college-trained social scientists and streetwise former addicts were recruited and given the responsibility of finding enough active drug addicts willing to switch from heroin to the more addictive but less satisfying methadone. Twenty years later the programs are still active despite what many experts believe are unsatisfactory results. The verdict is still out on this method of reducing crime. The addict in the street, though, knows how worthless the program really is.

◆   ◆   ◆

When I was a kid in the barrio, Lichi was bigger, stronger, and smarter than anyone else around us. Rudy knew him well and remembers Lichi as a strongman. He was a bully, but everyone looked up to him. He was not a leader; he ruled the streets where we hung out with ruthlessness, and he had no conscience.

Yet he sometimes did things that made you question his manhood. He was very unpredictable. I saw him in street fights with the guys from Hollywood Barrio when he was calling out their leaders, saying, "I want you." Then he'd kick their asses. I've also seen him run away. Lichi always did what was best for Lichi. He didn't give a damn how it looked to others.

He was a handsome bastard, still is. He had a way with women, and he used them to his best advantage even if it meant hooking them on drugs to get his way. His troubles with the law began early, and so did his drug addiction. He blames his habit on a bullet wound he got while running from a police officer when he was a teenager. But we all knew Lichi was hooked long before the bullet wound and the painkillers in the hospital.

I'd always known about Lichi, though we weren't friends back then. After I became a cop, all my dealings with Lichi were colored by the reputation he carried when we were kids. He was a challenge to me, the big man. But the big man was wrong, my way was better, and now I had a badge. We were on opposite sides of the fence, but we had an understanding. I warned Lichi that if he kept on the way he was going, I would catch him. I didn't want hard feelings, I wanted him to raise my right arm in victory if I busted him. "Arturo," Lichi said, "you've got a deal."

Our understanding survived the years, and the bully on the streets of my boyhood was welcome in my home when I asked him to talk to me about his involvement with drugs. The big man had spent most of his life in prison. When I asked him when he had fixed last, he said without hesitation it was six months ago. Yet as we talked, he nodded out to the point his chin was almost touching his chest. There were long pauses in our conversation when he drifted into sleep. He would wake up, raise his head, and say the first thing that came into his mind.

Lichi swears he is not a drug dealer, he will admit that he still uses now and then, and almost in the same breath he warns me that drug addicts are liars who will do anything to get what they want.

I had run into Lichi one day by chance. The barbershop had just started to get busy when he walked in for a trim. It had been over thirty years since we had seen each other. Lichi had gone to prison, I had quit the Sheriff's Department narcotics division. He looked the same, just older, with strings of gray creeping into the black mane of hair he always combed so meticulously. The eyes were the same, still wary, alert, picking up on everything around him, checking out everyone's body language. Lessons learned behind bars.

He had become very articulate. It was obvious he hadn't wasted his time while in prison. He told me that he went to every class he could sign up for and finished high school. We talked about old times as if we were classmates at a school reunion. He said he wanted to set some things straight. He wanted to put the past behind him and rid himself of it.

Lichi was released from the Arizona State Prison at Florence in 1984, after serving five years and three months to the day. He never received one day of good time. He did what they call flat time or hard time, no time off for good behavior. Everybody who goes to prison insists he's innocent, and Lichi also claims he was.

✚ On my last conviction I was accused of selling heroin to an undercover police agent. But I never sold anything to the ones who testified against me. I don't even know who they were, never have seen them in my life. Believe me, if I had sold them anything, I would know them. But then, I had a lot of prior convictions behind me for doing the same thing, and when I was living in San Jose, California, they said they had me cold on a sting operation. They had a video of my car driving into a barn where they were buying stolen television sets. At first they wanted to plea-bargain with me for twenty-eight years, but I held out until they went down to five years and threw in the California charges to boot. That way I could serve the three years San Jose was going to give me at the same time.

It was hard to believe how much things had changed since 1977 when I went to California and then to prison. It used to be just heroin and marijuana—that was it. Now they have these new drugs like crack. Cocaine is the most popular of all, but the kids are using this crack shit. In my day the drugs were all in the ghettos and the barrios, but not anymore. Now it's into the middle class and even the rich. When it was just the Mexicans and the blacks, they just threw us in jail, but once the middle class got involved, they started programs for them so they could kick the habit.

Before, when an addict was hooked and went to jail, the person just had to kick cold turkey. Now they will at least give you some kind of medication to help you through that first day or two. Another thing that's changed: We used to be able to buy what they called nickel bags or papers for five dollars, which was about a quarter-gram of heroin. Now you can't find anything for less than twenty dollars.

The first time I remember using drugs was when I got shot in 1954 by a police officer. I was just a kid, around eighteen at the time. Anyway, I ran from this cop in South Tucson and he shot me. At the hospital, any time I was in pain, the nurse would come along and give me morphine, and that's when I found out how good it was. When I was released from the hospital, I was introduced to street drugs in a strange way. It happened the day my wife died of a disease called lupus. She was just twenty years old and I had just been released from the hospital myself after the shooting. The doctor told me she was going to be all right and said I could take her home the next morning. The next morning when I went for her, she was dead. Her mother was at the hospital when it happened. She always blamed me for what happened. She said I had poisoned her, that I had murdered her.

My dad helped me with the funeral expenses, and I remember when we were coming home from the cemetery, I was crying, and my dad told me that it was all right to cry. I told him to leave me at the corner of Congress and Main so I could walk home through the barrio. I had hoped this would help me think things out. My wife's name was Grace Brown, and she was beautiful. We had two children, and we were very young when we were married. We got married through the church and everything. I never see the kids, they don't look for me, and I don't bother them.

That day I met Katy. She had just got out of prison, and we started walking together. I enjoyed talking to her even though she was older than I was. We just seemed to get along. That same day she introduced me to opium. We went to her connection right there in Sabino Alley. She took me inside, gave them some money, and they handed her a little piece of paper with some black stuff on it. I was getting excited because it was something new to me. She asked me if I wanted a little taste.

Katy stuck the needle in my vein. Right away I got a rush, and a few minutes later I started throwing up. I didn't like it, I couldn't hold anything in my stomach. I thought, what kind of a kick is this? Then she told me that she gave me too much, that next time it would be better. We stayed together for three days and three nights in a sleazy motel on the South Side called "The Paradise." I threw up day and night, all of this time . . . but I still put my arm out every time. Hell, it was free, she was giving it to me. Later on we went to Nogales, Sonora. She knew everybody there, all the connections. She introduced me to all of the important drug dealers and the guys who were using.

I used to bring opium across like it was nothing. I would put it in a glass vial and then into my pocket because I didn't know any better. Then, later on, Katy rented an apartment for us, and right away all these guys started coming over and she would sell some opium to them. When we had enough money, I would take her to Nogales again and buy some more opium. All this time I was the one passing the shit back over. One day they stopped me at the border and they were going to search me in this little room. I had the opium wrapped in a condom so I just threw it into my mouth and swallowed it. But the man caught me and took me to the hospital to have me X-rayed. In those days we didn't have any civil rights. They didn't ask if I wanted a lawyer or read me my rights. They just told you what you were going to do. But I got lucky. They couldn't detect anything in my stomach and had to turn me loose. The next day when I went to the bathroom, it came out. That's how the other *tecatos* [addicts] learned about swallowing their drugs before they crossed. Later some of the women started putting it in their vaginas. The bad part was that if the condom broke and released all that opium into your system all at once, it made you sicker than hell, and some smugglers I know have died when that happened.

In those early days when I was just starting on drugs, they used to sell the opium in *pomos* and *latas*, or papers and lids. A *pomo* was a little vial and a *lata* was a Prince Albert tobacco can. A *lata* cost a hundred dollars and it was full of opium, maybe two or three ounces. Now the cost is six hundred dollars for an ounce of heroin. You see, when I first started out, it was all opium. In 1955 all of a sudden we couldn't get opium anymore, and that's when heroin came in. The first heroin that we got here was brown like mud, and I guess it was good stuff. I personally liked opium because with opium you could fix in the morning, and that was it, it would carry you all day and all night. With heroin, in a few hours you were sick and needed another fix. Both are downers, but opium would give you a rush and you'd get a warm feeling and then you'd feel good all day. Another problem with heroin is that it's all different. You might have a connection sell you a paper that was very good quality, and it would last real good, or you might get some shit that was cut real bad and have to spend a hundred dollars just to get well.

I was born right here in the Barrio Libre of South Tucson. There were nine of us, five brothers and four sisters. We were poor, I guess, but we always had plenty to eat. Sometimes it was just tortillas and beans, but we didn't mind it. Now sometimes it's hard to even get that much. A paper of heroin in 1955 was five dollars, and now it's twenty dollars; the minimum wage was $1.25, and now it's $3.35—and people are starving. Let me tell you something. As far as I'm concerned, the environment where you are raised has nothing to do with how you turn out in life. I have eight brothers and sisters, and I'm the only drug addict, the only black sheep in the family. Hey, I've been married four times, and in jail half my life, but it's like throwing a cat in the air. How is he going to land?

My first bust was in 1956, for possession of heroin. I had just got my papers to report for induction in the Army and I had to go to Phoenix for my physical. When I went to the Greyhound depot, I had some papers of heroin on me, and as I went to open the door of the depot, I saw all these cops standing around. Naturally I thought they were looking for me and I took off running. I threw what I had on top of a liquor store close by, but they spotted me and found the papers on the roof. Later I learned they were waiting for someone else who was supposed to be coming in on the bus from Nogales. It was my first bust, but I still got two to four years in Florence. I should have got out in one, but I did my two years and got out clean. I was out for all of 1959 and went back to prison in 1960.

When the deputy was taking me to court for yet another narcotics bust, I was shot trying to escape from the courthouse. A very popular businessman by the name of Nick was killed by the bullet that was meant for me. The deputy sheriff who was taking me to court tried to say that Nick was hit by the ricochet, but it wasn't true. The bullet hit me in the arm, went through, and killed Nick. He was just walking by, and the bullet hit him right in the heart. The deputy was a new man and he should never have taken the shot. There were too many people walking in front of me. The poor guy had never fired his gun in the line of duty before, he didn't know what he was doing.

They only had me for two sales, but the court blamed me for Nick's death and the judge gave me twenty to twenty-five years on each count. It was a stiff sentence. I realized I was being blamed for the death of a very well liked public figure who was an innocent victim. So I went to prison again.

My dad had always told me when he came to visit not to waste my time feeling sorry for myself but to study and learn everything I could. He told me not to try to be a leader in prison, to mind my own business, but at the same time not to back away from anybody or be afraid. So I did just that and learned to read and to write, and then I started haunting the law library and learning things. There was this dream that came to me a lot of times as I was sleeping in my cell after my dad died late in 1963, about the same time President Kennedy was killed. In this dream the cell doors would open, not all the way, but my dad would be standing there and he would tell me, "Keep your chin high, Lichi, you're getting out soon."

I kept fighting the case, and in seven years I got a reversal. I was out by 1967. Everybody was really pissed off when I won the reversal, from the judge who sentenced me to the former sheriff, Frank Eyman, who was now the warden at Florence. The Arizona Supreme Court said, turn him loose immediately, throw Lichi out of there, the punishment didn't fit the crime. So the warden kicked me out of prison and didn't even give me any clothes or the money they are supposed to give you when you get out. They took me to where the new prisoners come in and literally threw me out the gate. I didn't even have the price for a bus ticket home. My lawyer had to come from Scottsdale to give me a ride to Tucson. I've made a little money in my time, but every time I went to the joint, I came out not even owning a clean shirt.

So I was free again, but only long enough to get busted by the feds. That's the way it was with me, in and out. I was out all of 1967, and then I was busted again in 1968 on another narcotics charge, and they gave me ten years. This time I was paroled out in 1970. First I went to Phoenix for a while and then came back to Tucson. That's when I found out my mother was sick. They had never told me that she had had a leg amputated. When I came home, she answered the door in a wheelchair. It was a real shock to me.

I went to work for the Hope Center on the methadone program in 1970. I worked there until 1973. I had hoped to be able to help people who were in the same shape I had been in a few years earlier—to get a job and to help them when things were going bad. The methadone program can help people, but it can also be a tool to control a certain segment of people—in this case, the drug addicts of Tucson. Now, the way it works, if you don't go to that group, you're not going to get any methadone. They get you up there where they can control you. I used methadone a few times myself, but I got off of it in a hurry. Mostly because I could see what it did. I had seen guys strung out on it who were in jail, who were coming off the program. *Hijole vale*, I mean, son-of-a-gun man, they were sicker than dogs. They were sicker than anyone I've ever seen coming off heroin or opium, and the withdrawal symptoms lasted a lot longer too.

At first, methadone gets you fucked up and feeling good just like heroin, but after you stabilize and get a tolerance for the drug, it's just like taking medicine, a drug you're going to have to take the rest of your life. Some guys get skinny, some get fat, and they seem to look older than they are. Most of them start drinking after they are stabilized. I don't know if it has something to do with the medicine or not being able to feel anything anymore from the methadone once you get to that state of tolerance.

I've had guys tell me they went out and bought some papers of heroin after being on methadone and did not feel a damn thing; other guys tell me the shit does work for them. I have seen guys when I was in prison who had been off of methadone for five or six months and were still sick and wanted to go out and get the sun and get healthy. Shit, a year later they were still hurting. They say it gets into your bones and you ache all over, especially your arms and legs . . . all your joints hurt.

By 1973 I had become a target for some of the people on top at the center. They wanted me out of the program, and the easiest way was to accuse me of selling methadone on the outside. I think it was because here I was, an ex-convict acting as a supervisor, and there they were with all kinds of college degrees, and I was telling them what to do. But I was straight all this time. I never once took anything from them. There were twelve counselors who were ex-addicts and twelve that had never used drugs but had gone to college and were trained for this work. In my estimation, both groups could do the job. It doesn't take a college degree to tell somebody that the reason I'm clean is I don't want to go back to prison because prison scares me now.

Hey, I wasn't in this just for the money. I really thought I could help others and at the same time I would be helping myself stay straight. I started out making seven thousand a year, and by the end of the year I was making nine thousand because I came up with the idea of a crisis center where a counselor would be available to the addict no matter what the hour. When someone was sick and needed help, we had to be there for them. When you get sick and you got the money, you're going to wind up knocking on the connection's door. So I said if this was going to be an effective program, why can't we be here and let them knock on our door instead of the connection's door? In 1973 I was still on federal parole. After I was forced to resign from the program, I went back to prison on a technical violation—I didn't give my parole officer a change of address.

I don't want to be that way any more. I don't want to be out in the street strung out on dope. I pray to God not to have to be robbing and stealing to maintain a habit. Anybody can quit using drugs once you get tired of going to prison, and believe me you will get tired of it. I've been married four times, and this one, Yolanda, is the best. I met her when I was in prison, about a year before I was released. She had been going to see a relative and I would see her in the waiting room and we started talking and became friends. She's not a drug addict, she don't drink or anything. Shortly after I got out we were married and have been married ever since. I would never again marry a drug addict or even live with one. Now my goals are a little bit higher, to meet better people than myself, people you can talk to. You know, people who don't scare you just being with them. Look at me, I don't have anything to show for all my years in prison, nothing to be proud of. Any damn fool can go to prison. Your close friends, you got to move them around where they can do you the most good. And your enemies, you just keep them right there in front of you where you can see them.

While doing our time in prison, the old guys like me learned a lesson. We learned about the law. We are not dumb, we get caught because that's the nature of our business. The people we have to deal with are not very reliable, and it's easy for the law to turn them against us.

That's why you don't see me with no son of a bitch. I don't care if they tell me on the street he's solid, he's dealing drugs, or he's doing this or the other. I don't trust anybody any more. You know and I know that if I get busted again, I'll never get out. I'm fifty-five years old and can't do no more time. You might think old Lichi is scared, and you're right, man. Old Lichi is scared because the man now don't mind planting something on you, sending an informer in to you, or sending in a brother, and they keep on doing it until they get you one way or the other. They know if you're dealing or not, or if you're trying to go straight and do right, but they keep after you and they have all the time in the world.

So now I have a police scanner and the book with all the codes they use. I have the whole thing, and I study it. When they say 10-45, it means to meet someplace, and when they have an informer in the car or want to meet with him, it's C-35. You're hearing all this shit and you sit down and think who's out on South Sixth tonight and who's doing what tonight. By listening to the police scanner I can sit there and calculate how long the guy they are after will last. Then I sit there and I can see my mistakes and what has to be done differently to stay alive. I say to myself, if I was him, I would do it this way or that way, or maybe pay someone else to do the deal for me.

About six months ago the cops called this informer on his car radio—yeah, the snitch had a radio in his car. And they gave this guy some marked money and told him to come to old Lichi and get an ounce of coke. I'm hearing this on the radio, can you believe it? So the guy says OK and he's coming east on Thirty-sixth Street. I hear him tell them he's turning on Cherry, and all this shit is coming over the radio. Then a narc comes down the alley and parks. So I'm sitting on my back porch waiting for this bastard, and when I see him walking up, I go out and meet him at the gate. Before he can say a word I tell him I ain't got nothing and that the guy that's parked over in the alley is a police officer. You want to bust me, man? With coke! And I don't know nothing about coke and I don't have any- thing in this house and if you want to search it, tell your cop friends to get a warrant. Then you're welcome to search the house and anywhere you want.

After this the radio scanner went dead, and I had to find the new channel they were using.

How do you go about becoming a drug dealer? If you're Joe Average, having a hard time making ends meet, and you hear about all of the money being made every day for just driving a car from point A to point B and getting a thousand dollars for a couple of hours' work, I can see that the temptation could be pretty great. It isn't that easy. You don't just walk in and fill out a job application or hand in a résumé. Somebody has to know you, know what you can do. You have to pay some dues first. Usually it's good to have a degree from a federal or state prison, or the job has to be handed down from a relative or a close friend of the family. At least that's how it is on the South Side.

For me, getting started was easy. A guy called me at home and wanted to see me. We met at my house and he told me, look Lichi, I have this amount of heroin and so much opium and I don't know who to leave it with. I want to leave it with you and I want this amount of money from the profit we make. So he sat down and he told me to get these guys to sell it for me. He told me to pay them so much, and so much is for Lichi. Now he wanted his cut from the top first, but it was still a hell of a deal for me. This was in 1955 when there was still opium and the brown heroin was first coming in. This guy was a chemist and he made it good. It just so happened that when he was ready to start distributing it, a friend of mine told him there was a guy who they call Lichi, who is pretty straight and won't rip you off, so look Lichi up. So he did.

I started selling, but I wasn't making money. I wasn't making money because I was a user and I was shooting it all. But I was making money for this chemist from Mexico—and right away we fall back into this little game we're always playing when we're young: We know it all, we don't want to listen.

There was an old drug addict called Moncada. That man would sit down all day long, and I would sit next to him because he had stuff up the ass, and I would fix him and he would tell me to take all I wanted. He would sit there all stoned and he would tell me what I should and shouldn't do when dealing drugs. He knew all this stuff from experience. He had been a dealer most of his life, and if I had just listened for fifteen minutes to what he was trying to tell me, I would have never been busted. What he was telling me was the wisdom of his many years spent dodging the law and being a successful drug smuggler and dealer.

Old man Moncada knew it all, he knew how to cook it, fix it, cut it to just the right percentage so a guy wouldn't overdose. The whole thing was right there in his fucked-up, drug-filled mind, and I wouldn't listen because I already thought I knew it all. We knew it all—and we didn't know anything. To Moncada and the old dealers, it was an art. He had learned from the old masters the ways to smuggle contraband into the United States without fear of getting caught by the law, the ways to cook the opium and then refine it to its finest quality for smoking or shooting. He was old and he wanted to pass this craft on to someone else, and I didn't want to listen and the other guys didn't want to listen because we knew it all. Now the kids want to be smarter than us and they go around killing everyone and ripping people off for their drugs and money. It's got to the point you can't trust anyone. To be a drug dealer now you better know how to shoot a gun and how to operate automatic weapons.

What this means is you have to be very careful, you have to be very cautious and keep your guard up all of the time. For instance, this young guy comes to you and tries to sell you some shit and he tells you he's going to give you a hell of a bargain on some stuff because the guy he brought it here for couldn't handle it. You look at the shit and at the whole picture he's giving you. Right away you can see it isn't worth half of what he wants. You think to yourself, do I look that stupid? This guy is trying to run a game on you that you used thirty years ago, and it makes you mad. So what do you do?

Most guys just get up and give him some shit and take it all away from him. What's he going to do, call the cops?

There are times when I think about it, if there's money in it, wouldn't I want to do it? But it has to be one hundred percent sure, and I got to know who is involved and exactly how it's going to come down because I don't need someone else as dumb as I used to be to take me to prison with them. If I have to go back to prison, it's going to be for a mistake I made, not somebody else's. When you get my age, you get that fear. Shit, I know how to die, man, I just don't know how to live. I'm not dumb, and I know how to work, I'm not afraid of it, but it's not the same as it used to be. Now you give a guy a thousand dollars worth of heroin to sell for you and you tell him, here, you keep so much and give me back so much, and he's all for it. He does real good the first time, so you give him a little more next time. The third time you give him more, and that's when he fucks you. Now you're in a hole with your connection. Connections don't give a damn if you gave credit, if you took a TV as a trade, or if you got a motorcycle. They want their money. Business is business. If you don't take care of business, they kill you.

Yeah, things have changed. In the old days we knew who to look out for, and you didn't have to worry about a narc parking next to your car and planting something on you. Now they use it every day. They don't like somebody because maybe he's wearing a diamond ring. Go plant the son of a bitch. Now the man tells you, "Why you driving a Cadillac?" Then you go home and you don't lock that Cadillac, you're going to get up in the morning, get in your car, and you're going to be busted. It happens, believe me. I don't know who they are, the metro squad, DEA, the county or city, or all of them, but they come, man. And when they come at you, shit man, it's all over.

Oh, and how about this? Before, when the cops came to search your house or your car or whatever, they came with a search warrant and let you read it before they came in. Now they bust down the door, put you in handcuffs, cover your face with a hood, and you're busted. You don't know who they are, who's searching your house, and you can't see jack-shit, man. They cover your face so you can't see who the informers are and whatever they're doing.

Look, I got out in 1984, and a couple of months later, in December, they raided my house when we were living on Thirty-sixth Street. They searched that house from three o'clock in the afternoon until eight o'clock that night. As soon as they came in, the first thing they did was handcuff me and take pictures of my face. Then they covered my face and did the same thing to my wife. They were all wearing ski masks. I didn't know how many narcs were in there, I didn't see a piece of paper or what they brought in with them. I didn't see nothing. They said they had a warrant, but they never showed it to me or my wife.

Then, after they had been searching for hours, just before eight o'clock, one of them said, "Bingo, book them both." Then they took us to some goddamn dirty place on the South Side and put me in one holding tank and my wife in another one. After some time, one of the cops came over to me and said, "Oh yeah, we're going to charge you with something else: receiving and trafficking in stolen property." Shit, I knew they were playing games with me. I didn't have no dope and nothing stolen in my house.

See, what happened is that they were sending people who they picked up for misdemeanors and telling them to bust old Lichi. Shit, man, the same guys were calling me up and telling me what they were being forced to do. These were guys that I knew, that I grew up with, but what else could they do? They didn't want to go to prison. All of a sudden here comes this guy and he wants to sell me a new television set or a VCR for almost nothing, and you know right away it's a setup. Maybe when I was a youngster I might have fallen for something like that, but not anymore.

But anyway, we got out the next day, me and my wife. Then the grand jury didn't indict her, just me. The police said they found some papers in the house, and they had, that much was true. What happened was that my niece was in the house when they busted in, and she had two papers on her. She got scared and stashed them. When it came time to take me to court, she came forth and told them what really happened. So they had to drop the case, and all of a sudden they didn't want to file the other charges on me.

I've seen them with their informers riding around, trying to set someone up. They don't care if Lichi is going straight, making it like everyone else, or at least trying to. One friend of mine told them I wasn't doing anything and they said it was OK. Give Lichi time, he'll make a mistake.

There's a lot of poor hungry people out there who will do anything to make money. For example, the poor *cholos* in Mexico—a big drug dealer will send a truck loaded with marijuana, and it gets busted. He don't care because he's sending five more trucks right behind it that are going to get through. He gives this poor wetback a hundred dollars and tells him to drive it to this place. If they catch him, what can he say? "Yeah, so and so gave me a hundred dollars to drive this truck, what can I do, my family is starving and I have to work." He has to take the chance. He's a wetback anyway. What are they going to do to him? If they give him five years or more, so what? It's better than where he was in Mexico. There's a lot of people who become involved with drugs because they need the money, and there's some who do it because they aren't satisfied with what they got. But not a guy like me. If I tried to start dealing again, I wouldn't last a week.

I don't go to bars or where I know there's heat. I try to stay away from people who are in the business or use drugs. I keep a low profile, and I still have to be careful because they keep trying to get me. The cops come back to my house to see if I'm doing anything, to see if I'm willing to buy stolen goods or get involved in the business of selling heroin again. The odds are very good that eventually they will get me, that someday I'll make a mistake or won't find the things people plant in my yard or in my car.

I have been noticing lately that an unusual number of drug addicts are dying from overdoses, and I started thinking about what the hell was going on and asking around for a clue. Leo Olguin was my friend. He was only forty-two years old when he died from an overdose last month. I'd known him since he was eighteen. On Wednesday he came over to my house, and on Friday a friend came over and told me he was dead. I couldn't believe it. Then I got to thinking that Leo's *compadre* Dave overdosed not too long ago. What some of the people are doing is shooting up a mixture of heroin and cocaine, which the *tecatos* call a speedball or a "Belushi." The heroin is a downer and the coke is an upper. See how much of a load they're putting into their heart? One is going up and one is coming down at the same time. I've seen them, man, they really get fucked up.

When I went to see Leo at the mortuary, he was all swollen, and I remembered the last time I talked to him on Wednesday. He was happy, he was driving his dad's truck, and he was living with him. Two years ago he found out who his real father was and now he was staying with him. When he came to the house at about two-thirty in the afternoon, I noticed he was drinking a lot of soda pop. He didn't come over the next day, but I didn't think too much about it because sometimes he wouldn't come over a for a couple of months. I heard that he had gone back to his father's house and evidently he fixed a Belushi and crapped out. His father had been drinking some hard stuff and checked him out but didn't think nothing about it. The next day he noticed he was still lying there and wasn't breathing.

Let me tell you what I think is happening. The *cholitos* are bringing in a better grade of cargo with a higher percentage of pure heroin or cocaine. Four or five of these guys from Mexico come in here and rent a trailer and start selling shit. Bang, bang, they sell to anyone who comes by, good stuff, all you want—and out you go.

The guys who know how to get the new kind of cocaine called crack are the ones making the big money right now. That's one drug I don't want any part of. It's really bad shit, and I have trouble enough with heroin. ✦

Lichi would like us to believe he is going straight. I suppose he is, as much as a man of his background can or wants to. He works part-time setting drywall and doing odd jobs whenever he can find them. The jobs come few and far between, yet he manages to own a house in a respectable neighborhood and recently purchased a new Camaro for his wife. He owns a motorcycle, and has two cars of his own. Besides this he never seems to need money and has a decent amount of gold jewelry that he claims isn't real.

The game between us never seems to end. He tells me he wants to purge himself and tell it how it was and how it is now, but never really unloads. From others on the street I hear that Lichi hasn't changed his habits. He still deals drugs and still uses heroin on a limited basis. He epitomizes the futility of the drug addict who really tries but never quite reforms. He is really tired of prison and swears he's not going back and that's why he doesn't want to use or sell drugs anymore. But give him a sure thing, a one-hundred-percent-sure thing, and he'll jump on it. He told me recently that he met Jessie on the street. Jessie is a junkie and a hooker on the avenue, and she turned him on to an apartment where some *cholos* were selling heroin. She told him the money and the drugs were right out on the kitchen table, and they didn't even have a gun. Lichi checked it out, but it wasn't right for him, so he let it slide. Two days later the *cholos* were beaten up and robbed and thrown out in the alley behind the apartment.

There's an army of budding young addicts all over the country and more are being created every day, auditioning for the part Lichi will give up one of these days. We still keep in touch, I see him on the street or call him from time to time, but we are still as far apart as we were when we were kids. Neither of us can or will ever change.

7 MAKING GOOD IN THE U.S.A.

My net profit is two thousands dollars
a kilo, so I make about twelve
thousand a week on the average.
Sometimes less, sometimes more.

—Freddy

THE MOOD OF THE COUNTRY WAS changing after the turbulent sixties and seventies, and as a nation we were starting to demand that the president and Congress take steps to correct the problems of drug abuse in the nation. At the start of the 1970s, a new menace was approaching our shores, a drug from Peru, marketed through cartels in Colombia. While marijuana and heroin were well entrenched as the drugs of choice among the blue-collar users, a new, more acceptable alternative was showing up at parties and holiday celebrations in the homes of the upper middle class and the rich. It was cocaine.

The demand for cocaine soared. The official word in the beginning was that cocaine was not physically addictive, and there was even talk about legalizing it. Cocaine became the drug of the eighties.

The narcomania of America was in the meantime creating another type of addict. For the first time the population of such countries as Peru, Bolivia, Colombia, Cuba, Panama, and especially Mexico was becoming hooked on the good things drug money could provide. Food, shelter, nice clothes, respect, and an escape from the slums or the jungles and mountains of South and Central America. You could now go to a remote mountaintop in the Andes or to a lonely fishing village in Mexico and find satellite dishes on the tops of shacks.

Drug revenues brought a way out of the hunger and poverty. Yet the ultimate dream, of course, was to come to America and make good.

◆   ◆   ◆

In the late 1960s the face of barrios started to change as more and more people arrived from Mexico, legally or illegally. The new residents naturally gravitated to the south side of Tucson because there they were more readily accepted and they could find others who spoke their language. Those who were undocumented, illegal, could blend in and not be as noticeable to *la migra*, as the border patrol was called. At the same time, many barrio dwellers were pushed out to make room for the programs of Urban Renewal, and the developers and property speculators continued to consume more and more land for the hotels, restaurants, and gas stations needed to service new interstate highways that were usually mapped across the hearts of minority neighborhoods in Southwestern cities.

Just west of a Tucson barrio called "Hollywood," the new arrivals were buying every available house and piece of land, establishing neighborhoods on the farthest outskirts of the city. Some of them wanted to remain separated by a reasonable amount of space from the Anglo way of life. For others it just meant they could buy the land cheaper and didn't have to worry about building fancy homes to keep up with the Joneses. It was an area of open desert where they could still keep a few chickens, a couple of horses, and some goats if they wanted to. Many of the immigrants settled into the very version of a good life they had envisioned when they left Mexico.

In the late 1970s and early 1980s, a different kind of immigrant from Mexico started arriving to provide cocaine, the most seductive of temptations to the ultimate pleasure-seekers.

Now parts of the Southwest look like an extension of Sonora or

Sinaloa, where most of the heavy-duty dealers are from. They build or remodel houses with a lot of arches, tons of wrought iron, and tall patio walls of brick or adobe. They drive four-wheel-drive trucks with expensive paint jobs, large tires, and roll bars, or sports cars like the new sleek Camaro or Thunderbird. Gold chains, cellular phones, beepers, nights out in a limo—and expensive funerals—are the trademarks of the Mexican dealer. But just who are these people who go about the business of delivering a few kilos of cocaine, ordering a hit on a rival, or dispensing justice to those who don't pay up? They pass through our lives every day, sit next to us at restaurants, or pass us on the street, but they remain invisible until they become a name in the newspapers or wind up in jail or on a slab at the morgue.

Bobby is a drug dealer, not a major dealer, but that's not because he wouldn't like to be. I met Bobby four years ago when he still had a regular job at a used-car lot on the South Side. The job barely paid enough for him to make ends meet, so his pretty young wife, Sally, had to work as a clerk in a supermarket. Bobby hated it. In his mind the man is supposed to be the only breadwinner in the family. The woman stays home to take care of the kids. At the time, Bobby and Sally had three girl children and one on the way. Another girl would be a real blow, he told me. Now they have four girls.

They lived in a run-down, U-shaped apartment complex on the far south side of Tucson. The small, two-bedroom apartments were in need of paint and repairs, and the driveway out front could have used a road grader to fix the ruts that were a challenge to any vehicle's suspension system.

Bobby's apartment always seemed to be in a state of disarray. Sally was having a tough pregnancy and she was still trying to work, so she couldn't keep up with the toys and discarded clothing scattered throughout the house.

One day last winter I dropped in on Bobby and Sally to see how they were holding up. Bobby seemed very pleased. He had just made friends with the new next-door neighbor, Federico Bustamante, who, Bobby said, was well connected in Culiacán, Mexico. Bobby was happy with the way his life-style was improving. In a few weeks they were moving to a new house. They had just given the down payment to the real-estate agent, and it looked like the deal was going through.

Bobby was using family contacts to pick up reliable cocaine customers for Federico. Bobby's family have been drug smugglers and dealers in Tucson for three generations, he told me proudly. Then his face sobered. "I really tried to make it with just my straight job. If Sally hadn't got pregnant when we were still going to Pueblo High, I could have accepted a wrestling scholarship from San Jose State and would have been the first in the family to go to college. The kids just seem to keep coming, and bills pile up, and you get tired of struggling all of the time. Hey, I'm not complaining, shit happens, and you play the cards you get," he said. So now he was dealing a few grams of coke during lunch or after work, and life was a little easier.

Bobby told me about the new boat and motor he was giving himself for Christmas and invited me to his Christmas party. This was going to be the best Christmas they had ever had. I took him up on the invitation, and when the day arrived, I went to Bobby's apartment. Before I knocked on the door, I took a moment to savor the fragrance of tamales cooking on the stove and to listen to the sounds coming from inside. I could hear Christmas music, children laughing, and the murmur of people warming up for a party.

Sally greeted me with a kiss on the cheek. The small apartment was filled with family and friends, valuable space was taken up by a tree so tall the top had to be cut off to make it fit. A mountain of presents surrounded the tree and spilled over to the sides. Bobby took the time to introduce me to every member of his family and to a few of the guests. I recognized a couple of names from old police blotters, a couple from recent newspaper stories. As I settled in, I noticed a young man standing in one corner of the kitchen with his leg over a chair. It was Bobby's new friend, Federico. He appeared out of place with his light skin and brown hair and a shy, over-whelmed smile on his face. He was clinging to a petite, dark-eyed girl who was very pregnant.

At first they were all leery of having a stranger in their midst, but after a few drinks the inhibitions broke down and they broke out small amber bottles filled with cocaine, armed with built-in plastic spoons on the caps. Before long the smells of marijuana and steaming tamales blended, and I wondered if Bobby's kids would remember tamales smelling that way.

I made it a point to talk with Federico, and before I left the party I was already calling him Freddy. A couple of months later I conned Bobby into taking me over to Freddy's house so I could get to know him better. Maybe I could become a gentleman drug dealer like he was, I told Bobby. "It's a young man's game," he said with a smile and punched me on the arm.

When we walked into Freddy's neatly kept apartment, Freddy almost freaked out on us when he learned I wanted to hear about his involvement with drugs. It took a little time before he would trust me enough to talk to me about what it was like to be a Mexican who speaks very little English and makes a living by selling drugs in the United States.

There's a big difference between the way a Mexican Mexican drug dealer thinks and does business, and the way a "home-boy" Mexican American drug dealer does his thing. The Mexican usually has a connection to one of the drug families in Mexico and doesn't trust anyone but those within his group. Freddy proved to be an exception. He was willing to talk to me.

Freddy is a second-level dealer, which means he handles only kilos or pounds and only sells to a few, very select third-level dealers. The third-level dealer supplies the street dealers who sell by the gram, eight-ball (one-eighth of an ounce), or paper. The street dealer is the one you are likely to have dealt with if you're a casual or social user. The street dealer also services the hard-core junkie.

The first-level dealer is usually from Mexico, and he makes the most money. He has more responsibility—primarily to keep the second-level dealers supplied. But he also has to rent the stash-houses for temporary storage of the smuggled drugs and control the logistics involved in moving the drugs to their final destination. The first-level dealer takes care of collections as well, and does the hiring of enforcers to keep troublesome dealers in line.

The first-level dealer usually lives in the United States, while the patron, or boss, he serves lives in Mexico. At least that's the way the organization that Freddy works for operates. The independents don't count because they don't usually last very long. They take too many chances, sell to anyone who has the money, and either get ripped off by the locals or get busted by the narcs.

Freddy was born in 1964 in a tiny village just outside of Culiacán in the Mexican state of Sinaloa. Like most of the people of the village, his family was very poor, and when Freddy was five or six, they moved to Culiacán so his father could work at a steel plant. They lived in a slum area of Culiacán and it was damn tough to survive. Freddy can remember a lot of days when they had little or nothing to eat. It was in these same slums that he met Valentín Sierra Quintero, a distant cousin through some obscure aunt he never even knew. They were the same age and went to school together.

It wasn't until he was eight years old that Freddy started hearing about the mafiosos who were dealing in drugs. He was a child, and he was frightened to hear the sounds of gunfire at night and wake up in the morning to see a body still lying in the street because the police were afraid to come to that section of town at night. Drugs and death were everywhere. The power and might of the mafiosos over-whelmed the city and made it the drug capital of the nation of Mexico. The police were powerless to stop the carnage in the streets. It didn't take the people long to find out that greed was legal in Culiacán.

In 1980 Freddy decided he'd had enough of poverty, so he said good-bye to his family and left Culiacán for what he hoped would be a better life in the United States. It couldn't be any worse than the violence and hunger he knew in Mexico. With only a few pesos in his pocket that his mother had been saving, Freddy made his way to the border and crawled through the international fence at Nogales into the United States. Following the advice of others who had made the trek often, he made his way to Tucson by moving across the desert, skirting paved roads, small towns, and ranches along the way. He walked mostly at night, carrying only a gallon-sized plastic milk container filled with water, a couple of cans of corned beef, and a moldy package of corn tortillas he had found behind the Safeway store in Nogales, Arizona.

Freddy was one of the lucky ones. The first night out he dodged two border patrol officers who passed within inches of the arroyo where he was hiding. The big thing going for Freddy, once he made it to Tucson, was that he looked like an American teenager with his light skin and brown hair. Relatives took him in until he was able to get a job and get his own place. He even attended high school for a year. It wasn't long before Freddy found a job at an automobile body shop on the South Side. The pay wasn't that great because the owner knew he was illegal, but it was better than what he could make working twice as hard in Culiacán.

It was sometime in 1984 that Freddy and Valentín met in a park. Friends since they were kids together in Culiacán, they just happened on one another. Freddy didn't even know Valentín was living in Tucson. They sat around, talking about family and friends. That's when Valentín asked Freddy if he wanted to move some heroin for him.

Valentín Sierra Quintero is the nephew of Lamberto Quintero, the legendary Mexican mafioso who was killed in the streets of Culiacán by a rival drug gang in 1980. (Lamberto was so famous there have been corridos written about him.) In 1983, when he was sixteen, Valentín walked into the Sierra Madres where he knew people who lived on the ranches where heroin was made. He went into the mountains expressly to find some heroin. Through his friends he was able to buy a few grams at a good price. Valentín was smart, he didn't try to compete in Mexico with the established dealers. Instead, he walked the five hundred or so miles to Nogales, the heroin packets taped to his body, crossed the border into the United States illegally, and brazenly started selling papers of heroin in Tucson. He saved every penny he made and went back to the Sierra Madres for more heroin. This time he was able to take the train. He sold more heroin, saved his money, and returned for more again and again. Once he was established in Tucson, he started bringing some of his friends and family from Culiacán to work for him. He was now selling ounces and kilos, but more importantly, he no longer had to be out on the street and take the risks himself.

Freddy has been in business with Valentín for five years, and when he speaks of his friend, it is with noticeable admiration.

✛ When Valentín was a boy, his family was very poor and he suffered a great deal. There were many times when he had to go out into the streets of Culiacán and beg to keep from starving. Now he is a very important man. He owns several houses in the Colonia Las Quintas in Culiacán, where most of the mafiosos live and where the houses are very expensive. He doesn't drive fancy cars and he dresses very casually, but he does wear a great deal of gold. Yeah, he likes that. It makes him feel good and important to wear gold, expensive gold. Valentín is well known and established in the drug community of Culiacán, and he is only twenty-five years old. Imagine that. I don't know how much money he is worth, but once in 1985, in my small apartment on the south side of Tucson, he and I counted out almost $500,000 in cash. It was the money we made in a period of three months of selling drugs in Tucson. He told me that out of every $400,000 he earned, he had to put $150,000 back in for more merchandise. That's when we were selling just marijuana and heroin, so you can imagine how much he's making now that he's dealing mostly in cocaine. There's more profit from cocaine and it's easier to transport and conceal.

I was never involved in counting the money again because when the next time came to count, he did it at another house. He keeps changing the location every time. He never tells anyone when or where the accounting will take place. Like the time at my apartment, he just dropped in with his suitcases and told me he wanted to talk to me in the bedroom, and then he dumped it all on the bed.

Valentín was sixteen when he crossed the border at Nogales, Arizona, by crawling through a hole in the fence. I came to Tucson from Culiacán a couple of years later, but I stayed, while Valentín went home once he had established his organization. Now I have my naturalization papers because of my wife, who is an American citizen, and Valentín got papers in Mexico so he could travel back and forth without any trouble. I found a job as a body-and-fender man, and I was doing pretty good, considering I didn't have my papers then and they were able to pay me less money. But then I met this girl in 1984. We started dating, and we fell in love. We wanted to get married, but I wasn't making enough to support a wife and then, naturally, a family.

It was easy to find people who either sold or used drugs, so when I ran into Valentín, I told him I thought I could do it. Finding the addicts and the dealers was the easy part, but it soon proved to be much tougher than I imagined. Selling heroin is nasty because you deal with the lowest level of drug addict in the business. These are people who really need it and are usually sick when they come to you. Sometimes they don't have the money. They are desperate for the drug and will do anything to get it, even kill you if you don't watch out. Sometimes they want credit, and you feel sorry for them because they are so pitiful and have such sad stories.

I found out right away you can't trust them because they will never pay what they owe. Every penny they get goes for more drugs. So next time you turn them down, and then they come back and break into your house and rob you. It happened to me once. I turned a couple of guys down, and they came back during the night and tore my house up to find my stash. I was lucky they didn't kill me and my wife. Another thing that bothered me was they always brought strangers around to your house, and you didn't know if they were narcs or what.

In 1984 I was selling heroin for $400 a gram. It was the black gummy heroin you see most of the time, and I guess it was about the same quality you find now. Sometimes the heroin Valentín brought us was almost pure, and it would have been too powerful for the addicts to shoot up without overdosing. We had to cut it in half with acetone and a little water, and then it was real nice. I could cut an ounce of pure enough to make two ounces of good heroin. Naturally it was more profitable for me.

I sold heroin for about a year or so before I talked to Valentín, and he let me quit selling the damn stuff. I started selling nothing but cocaine and a little marijuana. I understand that today heroin is selling for only $200 a gram, and it's really good stuff. If the addicts are complaining, it's because the street dealers are stepping on it too much.

It was a real break for me, a promotion in rank, you might say. Now I only have two clients that I am responsible for. One is a Mexican, the other is Anglo. Between them they buy about three kilos of cocaine from me about every three days. They never come to my house. When they need some coke, I take it to them, and it is always cash and carry.

I work mostly at night, but I have to be available for them twenty-four hours a day. My net profit is two thousand dollars a kilo, so I make about twelve thousand a week on the average. Sometimes more, sometimes less. My connection is Miguel, who works directly for Valentín. He has about ten people he has to supply. I think I'm the only one who gets his cocaine on consignment; the others have to pay cash. Miguel lives on the north side of Tucson where he can keep his horses and have a few animals. He has a couple of calves, some goats, and chickens. The animals are a front in a way, because

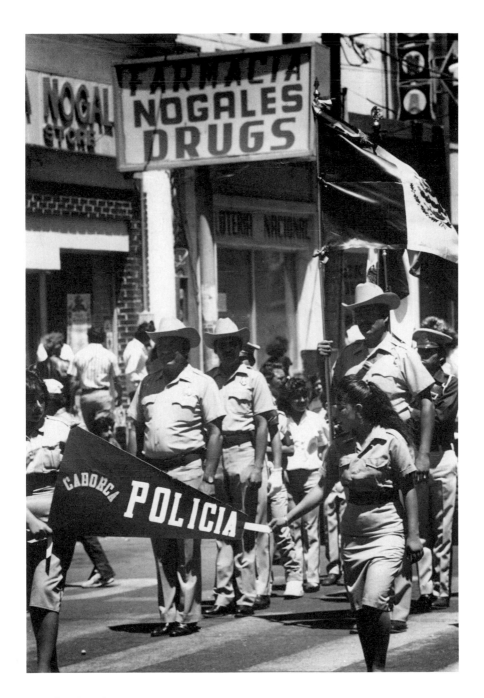

Nogales Parade Day, 1987

Colonia Buenos Aires, 1989

Pickup, 1971

Meat market, 1971

La Zona, 1972

The fence, 1989

Granny, 1989

Border gate, 1971

Seventy bullets, 1989

Happy hour, 1971

The connection, 1972

Out in the cold, 1980

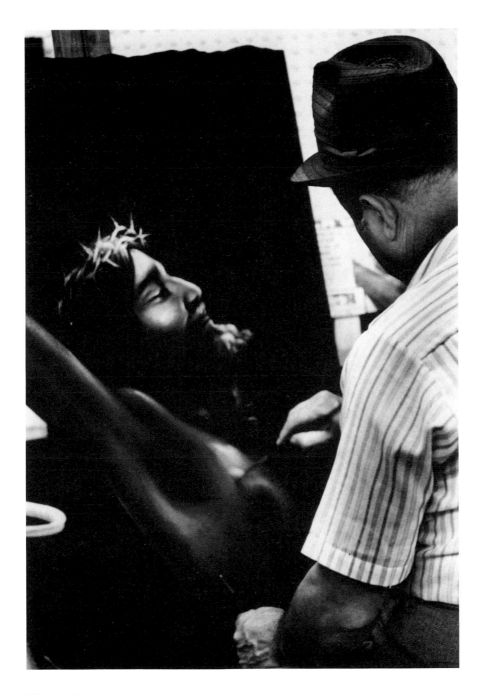

Black velvet, 1975

Day of the Dead, 1987

it's also a stash-house for the cocaine that Domingo, Valentín's number-one smuggler, brings in every week from Los Angeles. Miguel is looking for a second stash-house to store a large shipment that is coming in soon. ✤

For a few months I lost track of Freddy and Bobby, in one of my funk periods when I felt pissed off at my world, a world people apparently didn't give a damn about anyway. I couldn't finish one sentence, my computer lay dormant, definitely not user-friendly as far as I was concerned. Magazines that had published me in the past didn't want any more stories about this violent, drug-filled world that seemed to confront me everywhere I turned. But the violence continued to escalate. People were dropping from overdoses, five men were tortured and killed execution-style on the far southwest side of Tucson near the Indian reservation. A rip-off murder here, a revenge killing there. Two men and a woman from Mexico were killed in an apartment in a nice section of town. The neighbors reported seeing cars coming and going at all times of the day and night and suspected they might be drug dealers, but they didn't want to get involved, so nobody called the police. The killings barely got noticed in the papers and disappeared completely the next day.

There isn't a section in this city that's drug free, that hasn't had a murder of its very own. This you can say about drug users and drug dealers: they are not bigots. They don't discriminate against races, religions, or social classes. It doesn't matter if you're white, black, brown, or yellow, male or female, rich or poor, young or old. They still reach out and touch someone.

But what the hell, who gives a damn? It's my body, I can do anything I want with it. Most of us want to stop this terrible menace; we just don't want to pay for it. President Reagan put his wife in charge of the new government drug policy, advising the American people to "Just Say No." Now, that brought a chuckle or two from the drug dealers. And President Bush is trying to pull his magic rabbit out of a hat and stop the madness without raising taxes. He'll take the money for combatting drugs from programs for the poor. If this drug program works, the poor won't be able to use drugs to forget how poor they are. I was pissed.

I wanted to know why there is so much violence. I got back in touch with Freddy to hear what he had to say about the killings and about the people who have the power of life and death. In the movies and in fiction, there is always one sinister head who runs things, the boss, godfather, the capo, the patron, and everyone else works for him. He gets to be boss by knocking off the competition. Was there such a man in Tucson? Was the violence and the killing part of a scheme to take over?

✦ For the most part, I think the people who have come here from Mexico, like myself, do get along very well with the Mexican people who were born here. If they didn't, there wouldn't be so many guys from Tucson dealing drugs. The problem is that sometimes they don't want to pay up, or they even try to rip you off. That's when the Mexican dealers send their people to collect and take care of the situation. The same would happen to me if I didn't pay my connection in Mexico. Right away. I mean he wouldn't even hesitate if he thought I was trying to cheat him or steal from him. Valentín would send someone to kill me. It wouldn't matter that we are related and that we're good friends. If I didn't take care of business, he would order me executed.

Just a short time ago some guys from Culiacán killed a guy on the east side for five hundred dollars. He was a friend of mine, a white guy by the name of Randy, twenty-six years old. Three friends of mine had asked him to rent an apartment for them and had given him five hundred dollars. I know two of them pretty well from Culiacán, Juan and Martin. Randy didn't rent the place for them like he agreed to. He blew the money on himself. Randy must have been afraid of them, because when they came to collect, he was carrying a gun and he at first wouldn't open the door for them.

When he did let them in, he lied to them, said that he had given the money as a deposit and they wouldn't give it back to him. That pissed them off and they tried to scare Randy by telling him they were going to kill him. Randy was already scared. Juan and Martin are always armed, and when they saw that Randy had a gun and he made a move toward it, they shot him, but Randy had enough left to shoot Juan in the arm and stomach before he died.

The police caught the three of them a short time later, but only Juan was detained once he was released from the hospital. He is in the same jail with Jaime Figueroa Soto. The other two were released and went back to Culiacán. You see, that's what I mean. If Randy had not tried to cheat them, he would still be alive today. As long as you are taking care of business and paying what you owe, they won't bother you. I have friends in Nogales who learned this lesson. ✤

Freddy told me about Rafael and Daniel. They were midlevel drug dealers working for the Jaime Figueroa Soto drug organization a couple of years ago in Nogales, Sonora, when, for some reason, they failed to pay Jaime $300,000 they owed for a shipment of marijuana. Apparently they wanted to keep the money as long as possible, but, according to Daniel, they did have the money to pay Jaime, they did send word that the money was available, and they were going to pay him. Jaime didn't believe them and ordered his people to kill Rafael, the older of the two and the one he held responsible for the drugs. At the time, they were living on Calle Brazil in a middle-class neighborhood on the west side of downtown Nogales. The killers went with orders to kill not only Rafael but everyone in the house.

It was early afternoon, and it happened that Rafael was not at the house when four gunmen arrived. Daniel, the younger brother, confronted them at the door knowing full well what they wanted. He had one friend with him, but he was unarmed. Daniel couldn't back down, there wasn't any way he was going to show any fear. The *pistoleros* were not impressed by his *machismo*, they opened fire without warning.

They were armed with AK-47 assault rifles. Daniel took the first four hits from the heavy-caliber weapons in the upper body and was blown back against the living-room wall but somehow managed to stay on his feet. Bleeding profusely, he ran out the back door into the crowded street. The friend visiting the brothers was killed instantly by another burst from the AK-47s. Two of the gunmen followed Daniel out into the street and hit him five more times. It was like a B-movie—every time a bullet hit his back, he jerked forward and was lifted by the impact, like a puppet on invisible strings. He staggered under every hit, but they couldn't bring him down. People had scattered when they heard the first shots, and no one could help him or would even try. Daniel was covered with blood as he staggered past the tightly packed curio shops brimming with horrified American tourists. Daniel knew the hospital was just ahead of him and that he had to get there. He knew he was losing a lot of blood and was going into shock because he couldn't feel the pain anymore. Daniel doesn't remember walking into the emergency room.

For several weeks he was in critical condition, hanging stubbornly to life until they pulled him through. At some time before or during surgery a nerve was severed in his spine and he was paralyzed from the waist down.

Rafael was furious that Jaime Figueroa Soto could not wait another day for his money, but he should have known better. Now he was determined that Jaime would never get the money. Instead he used it to pay for his brother's medical bills. After Daniel was released from the hospital and was able to travel, he and Rafael went to Las Vegas and blew the rest of it in one glorious orgy.

Daniel and Rafael now live in Tucson on the east side of town, where they are dealing marijuana. Needless to say, they don't work for Jaime Figueroa Soto anymore. Despite being tied to a wheelchair as a result of the attempted assassination, Daniel is in charge of the operation. Freddy smiled when he told me about the simple but daring method they used to bring the marijuana to Tucson.

✤ There is a large section cut in the border fence in Nogales called *El Hoyo*, which simply means "the hole." It's just a couple blocks from the border-crossing gates and has been used by smugglers and Mexican nationals for years to enter the United States illegally. It is repaired every day and reopened every night. The Americans believed a surveillance camera was the answer. The camera and an attached spotlight sweep the area, making a wide arc and flashing a clear picture to the monitors at the Border Patrol office a few blocks away.

Daniel and Rafael studied the camera for a long time and found out that it always took the camera the same amount of time to go from point A to point B; it never varied. They rented a house on the Mexican side and another on the American side, each near the fence. As the camera turned, they had men waiting with bundles of marijuana weighing between twenty-five and forty pounds on their backs. As the camera went by, the runners were given a signal and they ran through the hole to the house on the American side and tossed the bundle inside. The process was repeated until the entire load was on the other side. Then the mules simply walked to the border crossing and went home.

Once the marijuana is safely stored in the house, Daniel and Rafael's people load it into vans. As soon as the vans are ready to go, a car leaves Nogales to rendezvous with a car leaving Tucson at the same time. They meet halfway between Tucson and Nogales to make sure there aren't Border Patrol roadblocks at any of the off-ramps on the interstate. When they meet, the drivers call the stash-house in Nogales, Arizona, to let them know that the coast is clear. They usually phone from the Cow Palace, a popular restaurant in the tiny community of Amado, frequented by the snowbirds (winter visitors) who live in the retirement community of Green Valley eight miles to the north.

When the all-clear signal is given, the vans leave one by one at timed intervals for Tucson, where the marijuana is stored in another stash-house until the buyers from San Francisco come for it. Sometimes the buyers are willing to pay more to have the merchandise delivered to California. ✤

Rafael and Daniel have fallen on hard times; they haven't received a shipment for some time. Nobody trusts them anymore because Rafael has a habit of coming up $15,000 or $20,000 short on his payments. He takes the money and goes to Las Vegas and plays the role, taking in the shows and playing the whores and the tables with abandon until the money runs out.

Rafael and Daniel have been lucky so far—they're still alive. Freddy knows of others who haven't been as fortunate.

✤ I belong to the organization of Valentín Sierra Quintero. But in Tucson alone there are a great many similar groups. I personally know of five drug rings that work in the city on a regular basis, and I know there's a lot more. Probably the best known is Jaime Figueroa Soto's because he was caught, some of his people were arrested, and it's been in all the papers. As far as I know, none of these drug rings are involved with each other. They each have their own connections in Mexico like we do. We know each other but never work together. Everybody does his own job. I can't speak for any other towns in Arizona or California, but in Tucson there isn't any fighting or killings among the drug rings over territory or anything like that. We all work where we want to and sell to who we want. When there is violence, it's because somebody tried to rip off another guy's stash or didn't pay for merchandise he got. Let me make something clear. Not all of the killings that happen in Tucson are contract murders. We are a hot-blooded and very proud people, so things happen and people die. Then, of course, you have your blood feuds that have been going on for years between families in Mexico. They spill over into this country because this is where some of them live now. These are just natural killings, part of life.

Valentín has had to knock down three people here already. There was a guy here who broke into one of Valentín's cars and took a hundred pounds of marijuana from the trunk. When he found out who the guy was, he ordered his *pistolero* in Culiacán to come here and take him out. The guy came here in the morning and was given a photograph of the guy, the address where he lived, and a description of the car he drove. On the first try the *pistolero* caught him alone and got the drop on him because he didn't know who the gunman was. He tied the guy's hands behind his back and took him out in the desert. Since it wasn't a revenge thing, he just shot him full of holes and dumped him in a deep well. None of the people Valentín has eliminated have ever been found, and the police don't even know about them. They just disappear from the face of the earth. I don't know what they do with them and I don't want to know. The *gatilleros* or *pistoleros*, or whatever you want to call them, who Valentín uses are usually from Culiacán, but sometimes it's people who work here in Tucson for him.

Valentín paid the killer five thousand dollars for the guy that took the hundred pounds. But this *pistolero* is very good and usually works alone, so not too many people in the trade know about him. Now if he had used three guys, the fee would have been the same, and the three would have had to split it. I know there are people who work much cheaper, ten times cheaper, but they aren't as good.

If the guy hadn't stolen the marijuana, he wouldn't have been killed. There are certain things that have to be done to prevent this from happening again. If Valentín had just let it go and let him get away with it, others would try to rob him, and it would only get worse. He can't let that happen. Now, Culiacán is a different story. I was there for a time in 1983, and they were killing two or three people a day right out in the streets in running gunfights. It was nothing for a bunch of gunmen in a car to drive by the bar of a rival gang, firing with automatic weapons while everyone inside ducked.

In 1987 there were fifteen hundred people killed. So you see that Valentín has to have his *pistoleros* for protection from his rivals. The police don't bother the mafiosos unless they get wild and start shooting things up in town and maybe injuring or killing innocent bystanders. As long as the mafioso stays calm and doesn't flaunt what he has, the *federales* leave him alone. Culiacán is the drug capital of the north and can be very violent, much more so than Tucson or any other city of its size in Mexico. ✦

The South Side streets are lined with dozens of new small businesses that didn't seem to be there the day before. They possess a definite south-of-the-border flavor. Especially conspicuous are the colors used to spruce up the buildings, bright serape colors that jump out at you. Red, green, and white, the colors of Mexico's flag, seem to be the favorites. The business signs in most cases are hand painted in Spanish. The only thing missing is the sad-looking donkey wearing a large sombrero while the donkey-man takes pictures of tourists.

I've noticed the neighborhood changing over the last five years, but the changes have accelerated recently. I know that some of these places were started with drug money, but I have no way to prove it until one of them is raided and large caches of cocaine, heroin, or marijuana are found.

Freddy and I took a ride, and he showed me the places he knew were selling drugs.

We passed a row of buildings and he pointed out a run-down auto repair shop that sells marijuana. A few doors down in a newer building was a Mexican video store. "The video store there—the guy who runs it drives a black Bronco. I know a guy who buys all his *coca* from him." Across the street, next to the truck selling white corn and green chiles for green corn tamales, Freddy pointed out a restaurant in a small shopping center. "You should see how much *coca* those bastards sell. Part of the gang is from Mexico, but the ones that are here started the restaurant just as a front, and you should see the money they are making legitimately in that small place. They sell some marijuana but mostly coke. They don't sell or do anything illegal in the restaurant, but they are doing very well."

The number of business places selling cocaine is staggering. I knew there were quite a few independents running around loose, but I didn't realize how much competition exists in just a three-block area. When the marijuana season kicks in (the latter part of September), they run around like cockroaches scrambling for a piece of the pie. Then the car salesmen, limousine companies, and all the legitimate businesses that drugs help to support start making theirs.

The faded crappy brown van converted into a taco-seafood wagon can usually be found parked in an empty lot on the South Side. They serve a really great shrimp, octopus, oyster—and abalone cocktail that's probably very good. Personally, I can't handle the cut-up tentacles with those mean-looking little suckers. They do make a great tacito with carne asada, a spicy grilled beef rolled into a soft taco shell. The three guys who run it are young, Mexican, and up to their eyebrows in the drug trade. The most popular item on the menu is cocaine, and if you have the right connections, they'll sell it to you right out the back door.

Bobby and I stopped by one afternoon to have a *marisco*, or seafood cocktail. We were eating the *marisco* under the makeshift canopy over the front window of the van. I was splashing a generous amount of a fiery hot sauce into my styrofoam cup when a Chevy four-wheel-drive pickup pulled up to the back of the van. Bobby motioned with his head as one of the guys in the van handed the driver two tightly folded squares of white paper, the familiar packaging for cocaine.

The young dude in the truck gave him two twenties and left in a cloud of dust. Later Bobby told me they don't sell large quantities, mostly twenty-dollar papers and maybe some eight-balls and grams. The three partners are wet, they crawled through the fence three years ago. As far as anyone knows, they have never been bothered by the law, they have a business license, and they meet all of the health department requirements. I didn't have to ask how they handle state and federal taxes. That's easy, they just don't pay any.

A few months ago I dropped in at the car lot, but Bobby wasn't working there anymore. He was supposed to work one Saturday and just never showed up. He called the boss several days later and said he'd been sick, but it was too late. It seems he had been calling in sick too many times and having too many personal emergencies.

A few weeks before, I had dropped by Bobby's house on a Saturday morning, and he looked bad. He was worried because Sally was giving him a bad time about using too much coke. He said that a few days earlier he'd been taking care of the youngest girl, who was just learning to walk, and had gone outside to turn off the sprinkler. When he came back in, she had got hold of nearly a gram of coke he had on the kitchen table and had spilled it all over the kitchen floor. Her lips were white from the cocaine, a lot like when you eat a sugar-coated doughnut.

Sally wanted Bobby to get help for himself. He said he didn't need help, he was in total control and could quit any time he wanted. Right now he didn't want to. About a month later Sally filed for divorce.

Bobby now lives alone or stays with his folks. With extra time on his hands, he has more time to devote to selling coke, but for some reason he has less money in his pocket and the coke just seems to evaporate up his nose. Some people say he's past snorting coke and has started shooting it with a needle. Now there's a guy with a gun looking for Bobby. He came to the house with his pistol wrapped in a newspaper and told Sally that Bobby better come across with the fifteen hundred he owes. No one has seen Bobby for several weeks now. His friends can only hope that he's hiding out somewhere.

Freddy continues to do business despite what appears to be a real effort by Mexican officials to stop the flow of drugs coming through Mexico into the United States. He isn't worried, the flow of drugs will continue no matter how much money the Americans throw into the fight. As one avenue closes, another opens. Of this he is sure. I asked him what would happen if drugs were legalized in the United States.

"I'd be fucked; they would put me out of business. It's that simple. I just hope they give me two or three more years, and then I can retire and not have to worry or carry a gun anymore."

Well, I don't know, Freddy.

8 NACHITO AND THE RIP-OFF MURDERS

As soon as we arrived at the abandoned ranch, we knew from the overpowering stench that many people had died here. We searched the house knowing it would be empty. No one in his right mind would stay in this stinking, unholy place.

—Juan Diego

DRUG USE AND ABUSE HAS BEEN on the rise throughout America at every level of society. Big money is the prize and there are plenty of takers. The catch is that as drug use increases, so does the number of rip-off murders. Dominant figures emerge and seem to take over control of a barrio, a ghetto, or even an entire community. We observed what happened in Miami when the Cubans dominated the city politically and physically. In Culiacan, Mexico, the number of drug-related murders rose to over fifteen hundred in one year. The trend seems to run in yearly cycles, with a rash of murders and rip-offs followed by a decline until another dominant figure rises to challenge for control.

Since about 1965, the importation of hired killers from Mexico, Cuba, and Colombia seems to have been on the rise. Drug dealers could go to downtown Nogales, Culiacán, Caborca, or Santa Ana and buy a *pistolero* to be a bodyguard or kill a rival. With the right contact you could hire a hit man, give him a picture and a plane ticket, and fly him anywhere in the country to get rid of the competition or collect an unpaid debt. Sometimes the plane ticket costs almost as much as the hired gun.

♦ ♦ ♦

So the seemingly unreal world of drugs, the wealth, fancy cars, and big homes, the free and easy spending sprees, the mafiosos wrapping themselves in the glitter and flash of gold jewelry in nightclubs from Las Vegas to Miami—this all has a very real, cold downside.

The number of drug-related murders has been increasing dramatically. For some years the focus has been on Miami with its Cuban connections and on the big city ghettos where violence just seems to go with the territory. In the laid-back atmosphere of the West, the drug menace and the murders that came with it seemed to get very little notice until recently, when top DEA officials decided to acknowledge what many law-enforcement officers in the West had been saying for some time: In the last decade Tucson has replaced Miami as the center of drug importation into the United States. The full-scale killings actually started earlier—as Mexican drug lords made the first concerted effort to control the flow of drugs through Tucson.

The feeling in some law-enforcement circles regarding the number of bodies popping up in the desert around the city seemed to be that the druggies were just thinning out the herd. The news media seemed to go along with this theory. But who were these victims and why were they killed?

Rip-offs and revenge were probably the main reasons. A guy gets a kilo of coke on consignment and then doesn't pay or doesn't pay on time or just flat out steals it. So the supplier sends one of his *pistoleros*, and the matter is settled permanently. Sometimes a victim gets killed for something as simple as a personal insult. Or it's a matter of machismo or a long-standing feud that has carried over from something that happened between rival gangs in Mexico.

At first, these murders were just plain cases of robbery. Run-of-the-mill drug dealers can't put their valuable cargo in the bank and quite often can't afford protection.

In the mid-seventies a new and extremely dangerous element

joined the hunt for the megabucks offered by America's exploding demand for drugs. It was the young broncos who couldn't afford to pay for enough drugs to go into business full-time. They simply went out and took what they needed. As a result, people died. The established Mexican drug dealers retaliated with a vengeance.

We used to think of Mexico as the land that time forgot. Now it's the land that drug money bought. For three or four hundred dollars apiece you can buy as many *pistoleros* as you need to come and get rid of your enemies or those who have offended you.

Nachito: The Killer, the Victim

On April 27, 1987, Ignacio "Nachito" Robles and Carlos López were killed and dumped by the side of the road in the tall donkey grass west of Tucson.

A passing motorist noticed the bodies early in the morning. They were out in the open, hands behind their backs in handcuffs, their feet tied. They had been shot in the back of the head. They had been dead only a few hours.

I remember that the sun was bright in the sky, and though it was early spring, you knew it was going to be a hot day. The local paper published a picture of the detectives leaning over the bodies in the desert, noting that one of the men was Carlos Enrique López and the other man had not been identified. A day later a smaller article gave the name of the second man, Ignacio Robles Valencia, a resident of Nogales, Sonora, twenty-seven years old, a cousin of the other victim. Then the story faded from the newsworthy and was forgotten.

Ignacio Robles Valencia was better known to police in the United States and Mexico as "El Nacho," "Nachito," or "El Famoso." The first time I saw Nachito and Carlos López, they were lying on an embalming table at a local mortuary. Before being shot, Nachito had received a very cruel form of torture called "bone tickling," whereby a knife blade is inserted into the fingers or shinbones of the victim and the bone and nerve endings are scratched with the point of the knife. Nachito had also been severely beaten. Carlos López, Nachito's cousin, had been spared the frightful ordeal and was unmarked except for three bullet holes at the base of his skull.

There were the usual tattoos including a naked woman and the Virgen de Guadalupe on Nachito, tattoos you would expect to find on someone who has spent long years in prison. One tattoo, on his right arm just above the wrist, caught my attention. It was crudely done, a spiral of dots in a circle about the size of a silver dollar that seemed to have no starting point and no ending. The body of Nachito intrigued me. Who was he, and what had he done to deserve this cruelty?

The next day when I returned to the mortuary, Nachito's body was dressed in a new pair of Levis and a fancy western shirt with long sleeves and pearl buttons. He was being taken to his home in Nogales, Sonora, by family members for burial. A half brother, Antonio López Valencia, arrived to pick up the metal casket. He paid with crisp one-hundred-dollar bills. Antonio appeared to be very much in charge, he wore new Levis and a shirt very similar to Nachito's but with solid gold ornaments on the lapels. Around his waist he wore a fancy leather belt with a large, round silver and gold buckle that had a small but operable one-shot derringer attached.

The services for Carlos López were held in Tucson. The large chapel was filled to capacity. This was not a suit-and-tie crowd. Mostly they wore jeans, reptile-skin boots, and beepers attached to their belts. I mingled much as I would at a cocktail party, trying to pick up bits and pieces of information and gossip. I found a friend who I knew was in the business. He pointed out several people with his eyes who were heavy-duty drug dealers. They were gathered to mourn the passing of a friend, or maybe to celebrate the event. I wondered if the killer was there to be counted. The large chapel was filled with the fragrances of flowers mixing with the sharp smell of rubbing alcohol and smelling salts. There was an abundance of weeping and wailing. Stern-faced young men stood at the head and foot of the coffin, prepared to prevent any disruption of the rituals.

Outside, the men gathered in small groups. There was very little joking, only serious conversations interrupted occasionally by the buzz of a beeper calling one of them to work. The parking lot was filled with four-wheel-drive trucks complete with oversized tires and roll bars, fancy lights, and tons of chrome.

The next night the services for Nachito Robles were held in Mexico. The wake would go on for three days with many of the same people in attendance.

Nachito was a thief, a robber, a drug dealer, and a stone-faced killer who operated for the most part in northern Sonora and southern Arizona. He killed for hire and sometimes just for the pleasure it gave him. He came by the profession of assassin honestly. His father, Ignacio Robles Morales, known as "El Bronco," was a paid killer before him, and at times father and son were confined in the same prison at the same time. El Bronco dumped Nachito's mother after siring four or five children by her. This didn't bother Nachito. He always had great respect for his father, even though El Bronco hated him and only grudgingly acknowledged him as his son.

Nachito was a product of Sonora, a new model of human designed for the trafficking of drugs and for murder, without conscience, without fear of dying, living only for the moment. In his twenty-seven years he smuggled drugs, sold drugs, used drugs, and killed between six and sixty people. Nobody knows the exact number. Nachito worked for Jaime Figueroa Soto, the drug lord now incarcerated under a $50 million bond on drug smuggling and money-laundering charges and also wanted in Mexico for murder. But Nachito also worked for the Somoza brothers, known as the "Quemados," the burned ones (a childhood accident left the older brother scarred about the face and neck). Jaime Figueroa Soto and the Quemados were long-time rivals for control of the marijuana and cocaine markets in Sonora. Nachito worked for anyone willing to pay for his specialized services.

I knew that the place to look for the story of Nachito Robles was in Nogales, Sonora, where he was born, and specifically in the Colonia Buenos Aires where he grew up.

I knew I'd get nothing out of Nachito's family, so I started with the Mexican police, which isn't as simple as it sounds. There are several layers of cops in Nogales. You just have to know who you are talking to. There are the *federales*, the federal judicial police, tough cookies who wear black shirts, black Levis, Rolex watches, and who never seem to be without chrome-plated .45 automatics and AK-47s. They are the most feared of all the Mexican police. Don't bother to try and find out anything from them, a former Mexican state policeman advised, and do not, absolutely do not go inside their headquarters building. The grounds in back, he claimed, are littered with the graves of people who were tortured for information.

Next in order are the state judicial police, who are moderately effective and, for the most part, as honest as a Mexican cop can be on eighty bucks a month. Then there are the *transitos*, the highway patrol of Mexico. And last of all, *la policia municipo*, the municipal cops who direct traffic in towns and keep the streets quiet. Many of the officers of the *policia municipo* don't even carry guns because they have to buy their own and can't afford them.

The office of the prosecutor general of Sonora, the equivalent of our district attorney, is located on a side street in a building that was once the home of Dr. Flores Guerra, a surgeon of world renown. The house has seen better times; now it is chopped up into a maze of offices. Across the courtyard, in what was once the guest house, they keep the files and records of the criminal justice system of Nogales. Here resides what is officially known about Nachito. It is a chronicle of a killer for hire who was a criminal from the time he was fifteen until his violent death. It seems he never did more than eighteen months for any of his murders, and he sometimes killed two or three people in the same year. He would be sentenced to prison for murder and either escape or be released for some reason (usually his mother bought his way out). A few months later he would get caught for another murder and sentenced again. Sometimes he killed his guards during an escape and sometimes he killed his fellow inmates.

In Mexico, there isn't an official death penalty. Unofficially, there is a law called *la ley de fuga*, the law of flight, or escape. When the prisons become overcrowded, the warden opens the doors, and a given number of prisoners, usually thirty-five to forty, are allowed to make a run for it. Special guards are appointed to stand on the walls with rifles and shoot at the prisoners as they race for a line drawn some distance from the walls. If they make it alive, they are considered free of all charges. Nachito was a master at surviving this form of parole.

According to friends, Nachito's mother spent every penny she could make selling used clothing in Nogales and sold much of her property to buy him out of prison two or three times a year. The cold facts about El Nacho are spelled out in his Mexican police record: "Ignacio Robles Valencia (AKA) El Nachito Robles—born December 14, 1959, in Nogales, Sonora; his siblings are Luis, Manuel, Rita, Isabel, Antonio, Olga, and Humberto. Last known address, Rio Hondo No. 372. . . . His parents are Ignacio Robles Morales and Petra Valencia Garcia. His height is 5'7", his weight 145 pounds, thin, dark complexion, nose medium, lips regular, flaring nostrils, oval chin, black wavy hair, thick straight eyebrows, thin moustache, clean shaven, a free citizen of this state."

A few months before Nachito was killed, he searched for his father to ask him for what he believed was his rightful inheritance. It was common knowledge that the old man was dying from cancer. Nachito wanted to belong to someone. He still remembered how his mother's second husband threw him out the door and down the steep hill where they lived in Rio Hondo. When Nachito tried to come back for food and shelter, his stepfather would throw bricks and rocks at him and drive him away. There was nothing his mother could do, she had other children to worry about. So he searched out his father and finally found him on a street in the Colonia Buenos Aires. The meeting was not a happy one, according to people who witnessed the event. Instead of embracing his son, El Bronco pushed him away. When he heard what his son wanted, he pulled his gun and told him to get away or he would kill him. Nachito was furious that his father would denounce him this way in public. He backed up, hurt and angry, and started to walk away. Suddenly he pulled his own gun. Father and son emptied their guns at each other at twenty paces as people dived for cover. Neither one came close to hitting the other. They were men who killed with sharp instruments, knife fighters who preferred to kill at close range, to feel the impact of the blade as it penetrated the flesh. When the guns were empty, they swore at each other for the last time and walked away in opposite directions.

Paco is a bartender at the Fray Marcos de Niza hotel in Nogales, Sonora. He works the day shift at the small downstairs bar next to the restaurant. Paco is tall, well built, light-skinned, and has curly brown hair. He is friendly and always seems to be smiling. Paco knew Nachito and most of the family. About ten years ago, when Nachito had just been released from prison, he came walking up Obregon Street one night. Some kids were burning a tire about a block from the hotel. It was winter, they were trying to keep warm. Paco's cousin, Enrique, was there, and Nachito said something insulting to him. Enrique said something back. Nachito pulled out a sharpened screwdriver and drove it through the boy's throat. Enrique died on the spot. Nachito walked away, and nothing was ever done to him.

Lupita lives in Tucson on the far south side of town in a small but comfortable house that looks like all the others around it. She knew Nachito and his family better than most. Her house was an extension of their own, and they always stayed with her when they came to Tucson. Especially Nachito. Lupita was his confidante. He told her things he couldn't tell his aunts, because they were afraid of him, or his mother, because he didn't want to hurt her anymore. He told her about the killings, more than thirty-eight as far as he could remember. Some haunted him at night when he tried to sleep. Especially the women and the children. Most of the time it was just business, and Nachito hoped they understood it wasn't anything personal. Lupita knew him to be happy, always joking and laughing, the life of the party.

Nachito tried to scare her sometimes, but she was too tough. She could handle him and wasn't afraid of him. He believed he was born to die a violent death, that he was not going to live to an old age. He didn't believe in God. She asked him about the spiral tattoo above his wrist, and he told her it was the devil. The devil, he said, doesn't have a form. Did he believe in the devil? Nachito didn't believe in anything but himself. He didn't have time to worship, he would die when he would die, when his time came.

Lupita went to Nachito's funeral in Nogales with flowers so the family would see her hands were not empty. The funeral lasted for three days, and during those three days his mother could not find tears for him. Lupita wanted to see Nachito in his coffin, to touch his cold flesh, to make sure that this time he was really dead. Twice before he had been reported killed by the police or by an assassin, and each time he reappeared larger than life. He said he had nine lives, like a cat.

Lupita touched his face and asked him, "Is that really you, you bastard? Are you really dead? What happened to the seven lives you had left?"

The day he died, Nachito was very nervous. He paced back and forth in Lupita's house, going often to the window in the living room and looking out, as if he were expecting someone. He had hardly slept the night before. He and Carlos had to go meet someone that night. He told Lupita there had been an argument over drugs with these people they were meeting. Lupita told him not to go. He said he had an Uzi submachine gun in the car. After that Lupita doesn't know what happened, but she believes it was one of Carlos's aunts who set up the deal. She was afraid of Nachito, didn't like him at all. According to Lupita, the aunt was heavily involved in selling drugs herself.

It's very likely that Carlos could have saved himself. The killers only wanted Nachito, but Carlos refused to back out and leave his friend alone. Carlos told them if they killed Nachito, they would have to kill him too. The best one can say for Carlos Lopez is that his killers respected his machismo enough to give him a swift death.

I knew from instinct that the killers were very powerful in the business, otherwise Nachito's brothers would have already tried to avenge his murder. I'd heard from a Nogales police source that Nachito's younger half brother had shot and killed a man in the Colonia Buenos Aires just for talking badly about Nachito a few days after the funeral.

I'd almost forgotten about Nachito, when the news broke on May 27, 1988, that Jaime Figueroa Soto had been arrested on numerous drug-related charges at his $425,000 home in Scottsdale, Arizona. Several members of his gang were arrested in Tucson, and the government was confiscating cars, houses, and money in Scottsdale and Tucson. Another two men were arrested in Tempe, Arizona, in conjunction with the arrest of Figueroa Soto and were being charged with the murder of Nachito and Carlos. The report said the murdered men were also in the Jaime Figueroa Soto gang. The accused killers were José Alfredo Carrillo, age thirty-one, and Alberto "Beto" Ceballos Campana, age twenty-nine, who Mexican officials said were both former members of the Mexican National Judicial Police.

Carrillo and Ceballos were originally to be tried in May 1989, but after some delays and after they posted bonds, they were released in September 1988. José Carrillo went directly to Nogales, Arizona, where he and his family live and where he had operated a trucking company before his arrest. According to police, the whereabouts of Ceballos are unknown at this time.

If Nachito was as deadly as he had been portrayed and was

anxious about the meeting on the night of his murder, as Lupita recalls, how then were the accused killers able to get the drop on him? We know from Lupita that Nachito was packing an Uzi, and he and Carlos were no doubt otherwise armed. Either there was a betrayal, or the accused killers were damned good, better even than Nachito.

In order to find out more about José Carrillo and Beto Ceballos, I made another trip to Nogales, Arizona, to talk to an officer of the Nogales Police Department. Lieutenant Agustin Huerta has worked for the NPD for twenty years and was familiar with José Carrillo. Beto Ceballos he did not know. The information Huerta has been able to gather indicates that José Carrillo is now living in Nogales, Arizona, and has been seen of late with a well-known drug dealer by the name of Juan José "El Toro" Mendez. Mendez was given this nickname because he is tall and very large, with big shoulders and a powerful chest. He has long, straight black hair and an Indian face. El Toro is alleged to be an executioner for Jesús Antonio Somoza Frasquillo and his brother—the Quemados. The Somoza brothers are vicious killers in their own right and are wanted on several murder warrants in Mexico, but somehow they have for years been able to stay one step ahead of the police.

As I probed deeper into the lives of Nachito's killers, I began to see a bizarre pattern. I remembered the devil on Nachito's wrist. Like the spiral of dots, with no beginning and no end, the murders kept happening.

In October 1986, Jesús Antonio, the younger brother, known as El Quemadito, got into a fight with two men over some prostitutes at the La Conga Bar in the red-light district of Nogales, Sonora. El Quemadito walked out of the bar and returned shortly afterward with one of his people. They were armed with AK-47s. He opened fire on the two men as they stood at the bar, killing them both while the other man covered him. In making his escape, El Quemadito took the time to kill two more men.

On the way to Caborca, a city about one hundred miles south of Nogales, the associate who had covered El Quemadito at the bar nagged at him about killing the two men and wanted nothing more to do with him. El Quemadito stopped the car and killed him. The other victim was a young American tourist El Quemadito kidnapped and then killed for his car, which he then used to flee the country. The bloodstained car was later found by the border near Sasabe, Arizona.

On Saturday, September 22, 1989, José Luis Somoza, the older brother, known as El Quemado, was arrested along with ten others in the state of Michoacan by Mexican federal police after the officers stopped a tractor-trailer carrying marijuana in a hidden compartment. As a result of information obtained from the driver, police went to Uruapan and arrested Somoza and the others. More than five thousand pounds of marijuana, numerous guns, and five trucks were seized. El Quemado was a suspect, with his brother, in eighteen drug-related murders in and around Nogales, Sonora, as well as the shooting death of the Magdalena police chief in 1986.

El Quemadito was captured several months later in a small town in Nayarit after he kidnapped a young woman he happened to see walking down the street and was attracted to. After he raped her repeatedly, he apparently went about his business as if nothing had happened. He was apprehended the next day on the information and description given by the girl.

At this point the circumstances of Nachito's killing were within my grasp, although the scenario they presented left many questions unanswered. Nachito died, put simply, because he was a free-lancer caught between two very dangerous clients, the Jaime Figueroa Soto organization and the Quemados, both vying for control of the

Nogales drug scene, rivals for many years. Nachito had worked for both, and many others as well, as a contract killer. As the rivalry intensified, the Quemados offered him a contract on Figueroa's life, and Nachito chose his side. He was a good candidate, perhaps the best, for the job. His credentials as a killer were unquestionable, and since he had worked for Figueroa on occasion, he stood an excellent chance of getting close enough to kill him.

The question that will probably never be answered is who informed to Figueroa, who told him Nachito was coming for him? We know someone did; Carrillo and Ceballos, *pistoleros* on Figueroa's payroll, allegedly killed Nachito before he had his shot at their boss. Nachito was nervous about the meeting with Carrillo and Ceballos, but evidently he did not suspect they intended to kill him. Nachito was careless this time, and Figueroa managed to stay one step ahead of the Quemados, for what that's worth. All three now pass their time in prison cells.

And the beat on the Nogales streets just goes on. Carrillo and Ceballos are free, and word has it that Carrillo and El Toro Mendez have teamed up, despite having been on opposite sides for years. American authorities believe that El Toro and Carrillo now feel it's their turn to run the Nogales show. Don't look for any change in the way business goes down. There's no secret about what kind of men El Toro and Carrillo are.

Huerta showed me photos of two Mexican state Judicial Policemen who were murdered in Sonora in 1984 on orders from the Quemados. El Toro is the prime suspect as the triggerman. The bodies were bloated and stiff, they had been stripped naked and shot in the back of the head. Next to the bodies, found in the hills west of Nogales, was a 200-gallon oil drum that was going to be used to burn them, but the killers were scared off by people approaching the area. Burning bodies in an oil drum is a common practice of mafiosos around Nogales. The bodies are stuffed into the barrel headfirst.

The next photo, in color, showed a pretty young blonde girl

slumped to one side of her car with her head resting back on the seat. There was a round hole in her left temple and a terrible exit wound splattering bone and brain behind her. Laid across her lap was a young Mexican man with a similar bullet wound in the head. American police have heard rumors that José Carrillo is the murderer. The killings occurred two days after Carrillo was released on bond.

The Reverend Dagoberto Quinones, a leading clergyman in Sonora, complained that violence has almost become institutionalized in the Nogales area and said it is beyond the control of authorities. That these killings take place in Mexico shouldn't make us feel any better. These are the same people who come to the United States every day to practice their trade. They are absorbed into the barrios of Los Angeles, the ghettos of Chicago, Detroit, and New York; they do their dirty work and then disappear. They reappear in Mexico where they change names and identification as easily as you and I change clothes. Local law enforcement and DEA computers can't keep them straight, and even the drug dealers themselves have trouble remembering what names their *compadres* are using on any given day.

I suppose there will always be a cop inside me. I knew how Nachito died and very likely who killed him. I had discovered much about the men who were good enough to kill the best, but I couldn't let go of this fascination with Nachito, this born killer, this product of poverty, drugs, the border, or whatever other label we use to help us comprehend such a creature. I knew the authorities on both sides of the border would be of no further help. The investigations into Figueroa Soto, the Quemados, Carrillo, Ceballos, the whole vicious cast, were still open, and no one was going to talk to some ex-cop who now claimed to be a writer.

So I turned to Freddy, the young up-and-coming Tucson dealer I had befriended. He said he would see what he could do. A few days later he called and told me about a friend in Nogales, Sonora, whose family had taken him in before he came to Tucson. Juan Diego, he told me, was a Sonora State Judicial Police officer based in Nogales. Juan Diego, like many of the Sonora police officers, lives in Nogales, Arizona. Freddy told me he had talked to him on the phone and thought Juan Diego might talk to me if approached properly and cautiously.

It was a Sunday morning toward the end of September and still hot as we drove south toward Nogales. We were to call Juan Diego from the McDonald's in Nogales and he would come to meet us. Freddy wanted to talk to him first, to explain what I needed to know. Mostly it was to assure him I could be trusted.

We arrived in Nogales and settled under a fiberglass McDonald's umbrella in fiberglass seats at a fiberglass table in the outdoor patio area. We were a stone's throw from the international border. From where we were sitting I could look up at the Colonia Buenos Aires, a ragtag collection of houses that seem plastered to the sides of the mountain on the Mexican side. It looked peaceful. It was hard to believe that this was where Nachito had been raised and had caused so much pain and misery for so many people. From its tranquil appearance you wouldn't think this is where the majority of the drugs pass on their way to millions of users throughout the United States. The parking lot was filled with American-built cars bearing more Sonora license plates than Arizona ones. I have never felt more like a tourist and an outsider there than I did at this moment.

You get conditioned to the image of a Mexican Judicial Police officer as a menacing figure with dark hands and dirty fingernails, palms up and outstretched for his *mordida* (bribe), a pearl-handled, chrome-plated .45 automatic strapped to his fat belly. But as I watched Juan Diego approach from the parking lot, I saw a young man, maybe twenty-seven years old, heavy set but obviously in good shape. He was wearing white walking shorts, a white T-shirt, and blue Nike running shoes. Freddy warned me not to move from the table as he stood up and walked to greet him. Juan Diego had light skin, wavy brown hair, and a thick moustache. They shook hands in a series of hip finger- and thumb-clasping moves, which I have never been able to master, and sat at another table away from me.

I could see at a glance that Freddy was having a hard time. Juan Diego kept his face turned away from me and kept shaking his head as if he were pissed off. Freddy looked worried, his hands moving frantically as he talked.

To my right, a green Border Patrol van patrolled the street, the back already filling up with potential migrants. A young man and his girl, both dressed in black, walked down the hill arm in arm. The van stopped, and a tall, bulky officer jumped out on the driver's side with nightstick in hand. His partner covered him from the van. They loaded the pair up without even patting them down and went prowling for more.

Just as I was about to give up hope, I saw Freddy smile, and they shook hands again. Juan Diego walked toward the parking lot without looking at me, but his face was no longer tense. Freddy motioned for me to follow and we walked to the car. Juan Diego parked his vehicle on a side street, and the three of us drove in Freddy's car to west Nogales on the Arizona side. Finally he turned in the seat and told me his name. We shook hands in the conventional style, and he directed Freddy to make a series of turns until he was convinced we were confused if not thoroughly lost. This worried me a bit. But when we arrived at the rather posh new apartment of one of Juan Diego's relatives, we settled into a conversation that, to me, was surprisingly relaxed.

✤ Of course I know José Carrillo. Who doesn't? He was a state judicial policeman for a few years, and I got to know him through a relative of mine who worked with him. I see him, I say hello to him, and sometimes we talk about friends or about the weather. Other than that I know him only by reputation. There's not too much I can say about him. He was always pretty straight, I guess, when he was a policeman. Then he quit and went into the trucking business with his father-in-law, a man named Quinones, who had a small trucking firm in Sonora. One night, shortly after he quit the police, José's father was in a bar and argued with a man he didn't even know. The way I heard it, there was a scuffle, and he was kicked in the throat and killed instantly by one of the man's friends. That incident seemed to do something to José. After that he turned completely around. He purchased a tractor-trailer rig and started smuggling marijuana for Jaime Figueroa Soto. José started driving new cars, dressed very well, and was wearing a great deal of gold around his neck and diamonds on his fingers. He started his own trucking business in Sonora and in Arizona with more and more trucks and tractor-trailers for his fleet. This was in the late seventies and early eighties, when enforcement wasn't as tough as it is now.

My police friends in America won't like me to say this, but I know that some of the American border inspectors were looking the other way when Carrillo's trucks crossed loaded with marijuana destined for stash-houses in Tucson. This, of course, was always the case with the officers in Mexico. But what do you expect? My salary is 37,000 pesos every ten days. That's about $110 in American money. Barely enough in our inflated economy for food and a small, dingy place to live. That is, if you don't find other ways to supplement your income. The trouble is that when a young man becomes a policeman in Mexico, he thinks it's a license to steal, that his position entitles him to do anything he wants and take whatever he can get. I guess it's because our leaders and politicians teach us by their example.

Let me tell you one thing I know about Carrillo. He was always taking credit for murders other people committed to make himself more important. Somebody would be found dead, and he would tell everybody in the business that he did it. We knew it wasn't him, and after we caught the real killers, he would say he hired them. Of course, he never said this to the police. As far as I'm concerned, he's a pretty nice guy, but understand that I'm not saying he isn't capable of killing someone or that he hasn't killed people before.

This is what I heard happened in the murder of Nachito Robles.

A few days before the murder, Jaime Figueroa Soto learned that someone had hired Nachito to kill him. Since Nachito had worked for the Quemados as well as for Jaime, he was the logical one to do the job. But Jaime had to know for sure before he went after anyone as powerful as the Quemados. José Carrillo and Beto Ceballos went to where Nachito was visiting with Carlos López and probably told Nachito that Jaime wanted to see him. Carlos insisted on coming along, and they agreed to this in order to throw Nachito off guard. Somehow they overpowered them or got the drop on them and hand-cuffed them behind their backs and also tied their hands, because sometimes if a man is clever, he can get out of the handcuffs. The reason they tortured Nachito was to find out who hired him to kill Jaime. I don't know if he told them or not, but I'll tell you this, I would have. As far as Beto Ceballos is concerned, I don't know him at all. I know that he comes from a very respectable and well-to-do family. He is the only one from that family who turned bad. He is very well educated and very smart, but he just turned into a crimi-nal, and from what we hear he is a killer. ✣

Nothing atrocious that had transpired in the sixties and seventies could compare with what was to come in a span of three months during February, March, and April of 1989. It all started in Tucson with the deaths of a man and a woman found murdered in an east side apartment. The victims were stabbed several times. The man was from Nogales, Sonora, and the woman from Culiacán, Sinaloa. Five and a half hours earlier a white man had been found shot in the head and dumped by the side of the road on the opposite end of town. No connection was found between the murders other than that they were suspected to be drug related.

Then, in March, five men were found murdered execution-style in a shed on Tucson's far South Side. Police said it was the city's worst mass murder. The men had been bound, and all of them had been stabbed to death. Three of the five victims were identified as

Sonorans, two were from Arizona. A neighbor reported he often saw eight or nine cars parked on the property when he came home late at night from his job. He noticed that other cars would be across the street, waiting for those in the house to leave so they could go in. The cars would stay about ten minutes, then leave. The night of the murder another neighbor thought she heard shots coming from the area of the house but didn't pay any attention to them, she said, because that sort of thing went on all the time over there.

One of the men, Hiram Rodriguez of Nogales, Sonora, had been stabbed thirty-three times. The bodies had been placed in a shed that they built only three weeks before and lined with plastic to make a greenhouse similar to those used to grow marijuana. To date, the killers have not been found. Apparently it was another drug deal gone sour.

As bad as things appeared to be in Tucson, nobody was prepared for what happened sometime around March 24 in Agua Prieta, Sonora, a city of 70,000 people 125 miles southeast of Tucson, near Arizona's border mining towns of Bisbee and Douglas.

We were sitting in the apartment in Nogales with Juan Diego, drinking beer. I began to feel that he was tired of discussing the death of Nachito, so I brought up the subject of the Agua Prieta murders. Juan Diego told me that he was one of the first officers at the scene. When I heard that, knowing the enormity of the crimes that had been committed there, the problem of Nachito was forgotten.

Juan Diego belonged at the time to an elite group of state police officers assigned to special details all over the state. They were ten men selected for a highly mobile, SWAT-like unit designed to attack drug operations and to handle situations just like the one at Agua Prieta. They had been issued the most modern equipment the United States had available. Flak jackets, assault rifles, night-vision scopes, and the latest electronic gear. Juan Diego's eyes sparkled as he spoke about the closeness of the group and the loyalty they had for their young *comandante*, Rudolfo López Amaviezca.

✤ There are ten of us in the group and our chief. Most of the members of the squad are young but very experienced. We go all over the state, wherever there is trouble that needs special attention. Mostly we are the assault troops used to combat the *narco-traficantes* in their strongholds or wherever we can find them. We are the ones who go into areas like the Colonia Buenos Aires and slug it out with the drug dealers.

I was in my office in Nogales when I received the call from the *comandante*. The office, by the way, was formerly the home of José Luiz Somoza, El Quemado. The house was confiscated from him and taken over by the state police. My chief told me to gather all the men and the equipment and bring them to Agua Prieta immediately, something big was coming down. I asked him how much equipment. He said all of it. This meant the bullet-proof vests, the assault rifles, and all of the electronic gear. We left immediately, armed to the teeth and itching for some action.

Rodolfo López briefed me that a number of people might have been killed at a ranch owned by Hector Fragoso two miles west of town. I knew the man he called Hector Fragoso better by his nickname, "El Tombstone." We knew that Fragoso was a contract hit man working for a lot of *narco-traficantes* in the area, so there was good reason to believe what the informant, Hector Reynaldo Gomez, who claimed he had escaped the scene, had told our chief. Gomez later admitted that he had helped to round up the victims and bury the bodies.

As soon as we arrived at the abandoned ranch, we knew from the overpowering stench of rotting human flesh that many people had died here. We searched the deteriorating ranch house and the area around it, knowing full well it would be empty. No one in his right mind would stay in this stinking, unholy place. The informant knew where the bodies were. "In the well," he said, pointing to some rotting timbers by an ironwood tree. This was not a job we relished; we are men of action and a fast pace. This was work for the undertakers.

The well was deep and not very wide. To get the bodies out would take special equipment that we didn't have available to us in Agua Prieta, so the Americans were called in. They arrived very quickly, but to those standing vigil it seemed like forever. It was not something that needed immediate attention. The rotting corpses would wait for eternity if necessary. The first probe of the well produced five bodies. When one was removed, another would come to the surface. It was slow because there were spearlike sticks protruding from the walls, so they could go down and clean the well, I imagine. After the first five bodies we thought we had found them all, but the informant told us to go deeper. They brought in the grappling hooks, and three more bodies were removed.

From that cursed well he pointed to a large pit that had been part of a septic tank. All around us men were digging and searching, and always the terrible stench of death that even the wind could not remove from our nostrils. In the pit four more bodies were unearthed. They were lying face down, hands tied behind their backs. A layer of lye had been poured on the bottom before they were placed there. Then another layer of lye was poured over them, and then they were covered with dirt. At least two of the men were still alive when they were buried. We know this from the informant, who told us many things during our interrogation, and because traces of lye were found in their tracheas and lungs.

After El Tombstone's ranch had given up all of its dead, it was time to deal with the living. We started rounding up the usual suspects based on what the informant had told us. He, of course, was detained as an active accomplice. Slowly, the puzzle started coming together, and before we were through, we had a clear and accurate picture of what happened at the ranch.

According to the information we had, Hector Fragoso was possibly at another house he owned close by. We located the building, surrounded the area, and waited until dark. The house had large double doors in front, and when the signal was given, I drove my truck through the doors into the house. We took them completely by surprise and captured everyone in there without a shot being fired. In the house were the two sons of Hector Fragoso—Hector, Jr., age twenty, and Emilio, who is fourteen. Before it was over, we had detained over nineteen people who had knowledge of what happened.

This is what we found out: A quantity of marijuana was stolen, over 100 kilos, according to the witnesses. The owners of the marijuana hired Hector Fragoso to find the people who robbed them. Fragoso and his people, including his two sons, found out that a local musician, Francisco Javier Bueno, known as "El Musico," was involved in taking the marijuana. El Musico was picked up and taken to the ranch where he was tortured until he gave them the name of another man involved who had moved the marijuana. There was a long steel bar that ran from one wall to the next inside the house. They tied El Musico by the wrists and hung him from the bar while they went after the second man. From the second man they found out the name of a third man, and from him the name of a woman. The woman gave them trouble and wouldn't tell them anything—until they cut off two of her fingers. This kept going from one day to the next until they had captured twelve people. Nine men and three women. One by one they were tied by the wrists and hung from the steel bar. According to the informant, some of them hung there for almost a week.

Finally Fragoso had all of the people involved and he went to El Musico and cut him down. "You are the one who caused all of this trouble, and for this I am going to make you pay. The rest of the people I am going to turn loose, but you have to suffer for what you did." With this he took a large stick, like a baseball bat, and started hitting El Musico with it. Before long El Musico was dead. Fragoso's people wanted to know what they were going to do about the other captives. They had witnessed him kill a man; they would surely inform to the police. "Kill all of them," Fragoso ordered. They brought the captives from the house one by one. Some they put before the bullet-riddled adobe wall and shot them. The others they beat to death with bats. One of the women was pregnant and near her term. One of them beat her in the stomach with a bat.

After they were all dead, Fragoso went back to the house in town, leaving the disposal of the bodies to his men. Eventually he fled to the United States. When we raided the house where he was reported to be living, we found films that these ghouls had taken while they were rounding up the victims and while they were torturing them. Everything is on film, as if you or I were recording a birthday party or picnic to be shown later for fun and laughs.

The young Hector Fragoso's brother is the chief of police in Agua Prieta and visits his nephews in jail every day. He claims they are innocent, that they were not there and had nothing to do with the killings, but we have films showing both of them armed with *cuernos de chiva* [AK-47s], helping to round up and herd the victims to the ranch. What balls, to take movies of such an atrocity.

Another thing we found at his home tells you what kind of man El Tombstone is. In the backyard we found a huge black bear tied to a tree with a collar and a long steel chain. El Tombstone made it known to Agua Prieta police officers that the bear was ferocious and ran loose in the house. If any of them ever tried to go into the house, they would be eaten alive. They had warned us about the bear, and at first the local police refused to go inside. I was about to shoot the damned thing so we could continue our search, when it started rolling over on his back and doing all kinds of tricks. The brute was as tame as a kitten. ✤

Hector Fragoso, El Tombstone, was caught near Three Points, west of Tucson, a few weeks later. He hired the best lawyer he could find in Tucson to fight extradition to Agua Prieta. Five months later he suddenly changed his mind and waived extradition, saying that though he was innocent, he could provide information about the real killers. American authorities, probably smelling a fix, countered by whisking him to Colorado in September 1989 to face federal drug-trafficking charges. He was later indicted by a federal grand jury along with six others. If convicted, Fragoso will have to serve his time before being turned over to the immigration service. If found innocent, he will be turned over immediately to the INS for deportation to Mexico.

Shortly after *Comandante* Rudolfo López and his special forces returned to Nogales, the unit was suddenly disbanded. The *comandante* was transferred to Navajoa, and the others were given different assignments. Juan Diego remained in Nogales but was relegated to a desk job until recently, when he was returned to regular duty. It doesn't pay to do your job too well in Sonora.

Ten days after the terrible discoveries in Agua Prieta, a drug-dealing satanic cult in Matamoros, Mexico, near Brownsville, Texas, ritually sacrificed fifteen people. The gruesome murders included the removal of brains and other organs to be boiled in cauldrons, from which the cult members drank to become invisible to the police and to rid themselves of all guilt. The dead included twenty-one-year-old American college student Mark Kilroy, selected at random and kidnapped. Kilroy was killed by a machete blow to the head, and then he was cut open and his spine removed to make a bracelet. Some of the victims had been shot in the head, while others were killed with a machete or a sledgehammer.

The motives in the two mass murders were clearly different. The cult members were under the influence of their leaders Adolfo de Jesús Constanzo, "El Padrino," or godfather, and Sara Maria Aldrete, or "La Madrina," the godmother. They persuaded members that if they carried out the ritual killings, they would be protected against the police, that they would be invisible. The downfall of the cult and the discovery of the bodies, ironically, came about when one of the cult members ran a police roadblock because he thought they couldn't see him as he drove by.

The murders in Matamoros were very gruesome, but death was at least swift. The slaughter at Agua Prieta was cold and calculated, the victims died slowly. They hung by their wrists for seven days and nights, knowing they were never going to get out of this alive.

El Tombstone is said to have killed as many as 150 people, but subtract about a hundred of those and you're probably closer to the truth. El Tombstone is forty-six years old, and, depending on his trial in Denver, he may never be brought to justice in Agua Prieta. But even if he is returned, he may not be punished anyway. Juan Diego told me that El Tombstone is loved by the people there because he spends a great deal of money in town. They have written a song about him. "El Corrido del Tombstone."

The frightful thing about El Tombstone is that he moved freely across the border to deliver drugs and death throughout the United States. He was well known in Tucson, worked here on construction jobs, and we might have met him at the barbershop as he waited his turn to have his hair cut. We might have talked about baseball or boxing and might even have shaken hands with him. He enlisted in the United States Army in Tucson in 1963 and served eighteen months in Germany. He was deported in 1983, but he has been in Tucson several times since.

There are thousands of good people who come across from Mexico every day and contribute to our economy, and we benefit from the cultural exchange as well. My roots are over there, in the small village of Moctezuma, near Altar, and in Rayon, near Magdalena, where I still have family. My great-grandfather, Don Leopoldo Carrillo, first passed through here in 1849 on a wagon train, to settle in Tucson ten years later. He loved Mexico and taught his children to love Mexico, second only to the United States. This tradition has been handed down to us, and I don't write the sad stories about the people and the events taking place there lightly or without a feeling of sorrow.

EPILOGUE

THE RAIN FINALLY CAME TO Tucson in early October. It had been a dry year, the likes of which we hadn't seen in fifty years. The days were still warm, but the nights had started to cool with a hint that maybe summer wouldn't last all year long. The marijuana crop was just starting to trickle in, but prices were very high. Another cycle in the drug trade was opening as I struggled to find answers to an endless stream of questions. What's going to happen next? What do all the drugs and the violence mean? Where is the drug trade headed? I was suddenly sick to death of a world I had entered to write this book.

A couple of years ago at this time I had been in a remote fishing village on the west coast of Mexico drinking beer with friends in an RV parked on the beach. At night we gathered with the locals around a fire near the surf. We sang *corridos*—one villager had a guitar—and we talked of the day's fishing, of the near misses. One of our group asked, "Anyone want some marijuana?" It seemed like a good idea at the time, and a twenty-dollar bill found its way into the hands of a smiling kid from the village. He disappeared into the darkness beyond our fire, and another round of stories and lies started.

A half-hour passed and we had nearly forgotten the boy and the twenty dollars. The guys who invested the money expected to see him return, if at all, with a sandwich bag full of pot. When the boy did return from the darkness, it was with a garbage bag hoisted over his shoulder. It was funny to us when it happened. The guys rolled a couple of joints, the party continued, and at the end of the evening we sent the boy on his way with his sack of grass nearly intact.

What that tells me now is that drugs not only have spread to every level of American society, but they are readily available in the remotest corner of the continent. The Mexico I had known all my life is a place where *pulque*, mescal, and tequila were locally manufactured drugs of choice. Hell, I can remember a time when there were more drug dealers in Mexico than drug users.

It's hard to argue against the notion that drugs have changed the face of everyone's world. That the lot of the average Mexicans was so poor, their hopes so limited, and that the vast majority of them were content to take what pleasures came their way each day, is a proposition that used to hold a grain of truth. Today, however, the drug industry and drug money have raised the expectations of millions south of the border to middle-class comfort and beyond. A couple of kids raised in the most extreme poverty imaginable on the violent streets of Culiacán can, if they're smart and very lucky, retire as millionaires by the time they're thirty. Ask Freddy and Valentín.

The business is so big it provides images almost beyond our comprehension. Imagine a room the size of a master bedroom in a nice home, filled floor to ceiling, wall to wall, with stacks of hundred-dollar bills. The room really exists. It's in a ranch house in Mexico near the U.S. border. The owner of the ranch sells a hundred pounds of heroin twice a year to a dealer in Chicago. He never touches his product once it leaves the laboratory on the ranch. He's a small-time supplier compared to others in the area.

Of course, most Mexicans who choose the trade as their avenue to comfort and riches won't make it. In the current climate of drug dealing they're likelier to find a violent death. But they can hope, and that's something that I see going out of life north of the border—hope for a better future.

It seems to be a part of human nature to seek escape from reality. The only people who will never be tempted to a momentary escape are those whose lives are satisfying enough without it. The numbers of those people are shrinking in America, and that should be apparent even in Washington, D.C. A lot of Americans are swallowing the hard facts that they'll probably never be able to afford that house and that they'll have a monthly car payment for the rest of their lives no matter what they drive. A lot of them are ripe for that easy escape. Why not score a gram and feel like royalty for a few hours?

Another thing that should be apparent is that money and troops aren't going to solve the problem. Imagine a battle front two thousand miles wide, consisting of desert and mountains. Imagine that front under constant attack by well-armed and supplied guerrillas who were born there and know every inch of the terrain. That's how the war against the smuggler stacks up. Take that scenario and add to it the extreme secrecy of the smuggler and his culture. He learns to become invisible to stay alive. I'd venture to say that if we put the entire U.S. Army along the border with Mexico, the smugglers would still get through.

Drugs were here before there were people to use them. Drugs didn't cause the problem. Drugs didn't cause people to lose hope, but drugs are there for the hopeless. I could begin to sound like the cynic I sometimes fear I've become. I could say that the drug problem is leading to a complete breakdown in society, a breakdown in relations between nations. I could say that the source of the problem goes back to the individual or to the family, where instead of talking about our day we watch television and where kids worry more about what their peers think than what their parents think. I could say that drugs are simply a business opportunity for those who supply them, or that drugs are killing the children of those who demand them.

About all I can be sure about is that there is a supply south of the

U.S. border and a demand north of it. Which came first is a chicken-or-egg puzzle that doesn't seem to be important anymore. To put it another way, and to borrow a cliché from our last war, the dominoes are lined up from Bolivia to the northern border of Mexico. Which direction they fall doesn't change the fact that the dominoes are there. All that matters is that the country of my ancestors supplies drugs and the country of my birth demands them.

To understand the enormity and complexity of the problem I thought it was important to hear the voices of the people we are dealing with, to learn what they are like and why it is so hard to control what they do. The people in this book do not provide a reflection of the good people of the United States and Mexico, nor are they typical of the majority of Mexican Americans I grew up with. But they exist, and if they're willing to talk to us, I believe we should listen.

About the Photographer

David Burckhalter has photographed in Arizona and Sonora, Mexico, for over twenty years, with a special interest in the Indian tribes of Sonora—the Yaquis, Mayos, and Seris. His photographs of people and landscapes of the desert Southwest are widely published in newspapers and magazines. His book of photographs, *The Seris*, was published by the University of Arizona Press in 1976. David Burckhalter lives in Tucson, and he is currently working on another book project south of the U.S. border.